C000292047

The Happy Financial Adviser

Andrew Goodwin

RƎTHINK PRESS

First published in Great Britain 2017 by Rethink Press (www.rethinkpress.com)

Cover image © Adobe Stock / Neyro
Illustrations by Tim Kenning

Contents

For
Catherine and Thomas

I dedicate this book to all those financial advisers who want to make a difference in the lives of others.

Be happy.

Foreword

I have known and worked closely with Andrew for many years now, and what is certain is that he puts into action his own words, so this book has meaning.

He clearly sets out what is important not only for financial advisers, but indeed anyone whose prosperity ultimately depends on making others wealthier because of their actions. As he states, success doesn't have to lead to happiness, but happiness in your job is a certain requirement for long term success. So, if the adviser is happy in themselves they are much more likely to be successful.

I believe this view is true, and is also great news as recent changes in the market mean that the need for trusted, and happy advisers is greater than ever, and of course there are fewer advisers than ever before. A growing and huge existing consumer market, but a diminishing ability to service it means that the right adviser, in the right environment, will do well.

A perfect opportunity exists for advisers to join together (in order to share specialisms) who will 'sit on the same side of the table' as the client. More than anything else that is what a client needs, and if that makes the adviser happy, and it does so for the vast majority, then much greater success will be achieved.

The client needs impartiality from the adviser, their problem seen through the emotions of the client, together with the objectivity and specialism of an impartial adviser.

The cost of providing advice and an ongoing relationship is key. Andrew's extensive use of technology in doing this is crucial. He plays to the specialism of his firm in providing the right home for advisers, who in turn give good advice to clients; but uses others to put in place other specialities such as internet based technology so his clients have their details at their fingertips, always.

Andrew has always had a strong vision of what he believes in, and this book is a fantastic advert for that vision – enjoy!

David Harrison
Managing Partner, True Potential LLP

Introduction

Why do so many financial advisers appear to be unhappy and how do you change that? It's a natural assumption that if you work hard and earn plenty of money you will achieve success, and further, that success will lead to happiness.

However, psychological studies show that happiness doesn't necessarily follow success. In fact, this formula of 'success leading to happiness' is the wrong way around and in fact, the opposite is true: it is happiness that leads to success.

Happiness does not need to be set aside as some emotional response to future achievement, you can work at being happy right now. If you accept that happiness can be achieved through a change in the way you work, then as a financial adviser you are best placed to achieve happiness for you and your clients. Happiness is not just achieved with yet more income but instead connecting with new clients, having the freedom to be yourself and making a positive difference in the lives of others.

Barriers to happiness

The industry regulators, the decision makers, the professional indemnity insurers and other institutions that make up the financial advice industry, are seen by many unhappy financial advisers today as a barrier to business and progress, but in fact, this does not have to be the case.

You are overworked, underpaid and stressed to bursting point, but I have a solution. I believe it is the right time for independent financial advisers to take back control and become the key ambassadors of financial advice and financial happiness. Threats to your very existence are real, scary and happening right now. It is important than ever before that we establish better ways of working.

I want you, today's financial adviser, to take back control of the Financial Services market and you can achieve this by better understanding where you and the industry are now. To know the choices you can make and commit to change. To let go of the old traditional concepts and make sure you embrace ambition by using the latest technology. To shout louder and influence industry changes through structured self-development, personal promotion through the medium of social media and to focus on client outcomes instead of products.

I want to change the way financial advice is perceived by the general public, and my route to that outcome is to restore credibility to the industry. This can be achieved by focusing on what the financial advisers can do now to make their life easier, more pleasurable and happier.

When you look deep enough and investigate what is actually happening, then all you will see is an opportunity. When financial adviser numbers are reducing, viewed with a serious undertone of concern for the people that keep this industry alive, then a happy and more positive outlook is needed.

You need to know the problem areas and threats to your very existence, introduce new ways of working which will make a positive difference. My aim is to focus your attention to first achieve a happier working day, by taking the necessary steps to ensure a secure future exists for you. The old way is not the way to survive. Tradition without ambition is stagnation!

Who should read this book?

This book is aimed at experienced financial advisers who already have clients and simply need support, simplicity, and future security. The focus is on your business structure and strategy, your credibility, and marketing your own profile. Equally, you do not need to give up your 'un-profitable' clients or redirect your focus towards particular clients; this is about ensuring you can continue to provide financial advice for everyone.

By following my 6S (Success) journey, you can be directly authorised without the burden, independent without the research demands, supported without the costs and provide a modern and ambitious client service without losing tradition. It's about helping people.

I will take you to a point where you are ready for solutions and willing to adapt to new surroundings, keen to be happy again; as fresh as you were on the first day you entered this industry, expectant, enthusiastic and willing to learn.

Why I've written this book

I have worked in this industry for over twenty years, and have gained valuable experience on how financial advice is distributed across the UK. I have seen changing business models and changing technology and survived many severe changes when many others have failed.

Since 2004 I have worked closely with financial advisers from all backgrounds; Banks, Life companies, small IFA practices, and networks advisers. I have worked with Firm Principals, Directors and partners of Directly Authorised firms who have had enough of the regulatory administration. I have interviewed, persuaded, moved, changed, supported, supervised, influenced and sadly, on occasion, sacked!

Frustrated by the industry direction, I decided to set up my own company that would deliver what I believe all clients want; unbiased and unrestricted financial advice and provided under a brand that clients could easily understand.

Having worked with a very successful UK National firm, I transferred my knowledge and skills to my own firm which I set up in 2010. Called Truly Independent Ltd, I wanted it to make a positive difference. First and foremost, with the threat of the Retail Distribution Review (RDR 1 January 2013) changing the face of our industry, I wanted to make sure clients always have access to independent financial advice. I wanted to ensure clients understood that there was a brand with a common thread throughout the company and that no matter who you spoke to from our Firm, from anywhere in the Country, clients would get consistent quality *truly* independent financial advice. Everything we do is with the client in mind, and this book is no different.

Read on if, like me, you live to be happy.

For Greater Financial Success, First Embrace Happiness

'Success is not the key to happiness.
Happiness is the key to success.
If you love what you are doing,
you will be successful.'
Albert Schweitzer
Theologian, philosopher, and physician.

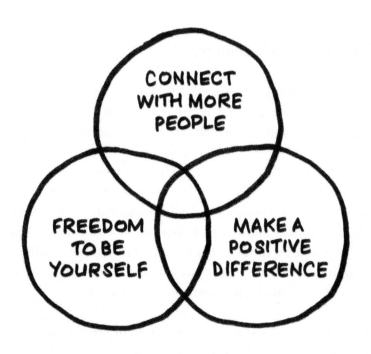

In truth, any successful business has strong principles at the core; an ethos, a concept or idea from which excellent ideas can develop. Ideas without evidence are just theories and postulation. Any assumption is guessing without basis. We live by the way we have been taught and as a result will often assume things without question.

In this section, I will explore the fundamental determinants required to create a strong foundation in business and the essence of happiness. You need no longer expect, there is no reason to wait, and you can no longer assume. Take the time to open your mind and let your imagination flow.

The happy determinants

As we explored in the introduction, it's a natural assumption that if you work hard and earn plenty of money, you will achieve success, which will lead to happiness.

The world is full of people striving for success, putting long hours into their work in the hope of achieving that success and the happiness it will bring. However, psychological studies show that happiness doesn't necessarily follow success. In fact, this formula of 'success leading to happiness' is the wrong way around and in fact, the opposite is true. Happiness leads to success.

Happiness is seen by many as an emotional response to achieving financial success, and it is no wonder since we are taught this at school. We are shown, if you work hard at passing your exams, achieve good qualifications, go to University to obtain a degree in a recognised profession or attend College to gain a much-needed skill, then you will be successful. At no point are we taught about happiness, yet we all seek it.

Recent university research delivers strong evidence that individuals who are happier are approximately 12% more productive. ('Happiness and Productivity', University of Warwick UK, 10th Feb 2014). This research is available via our website www.happyfinancialadvisers.co.uk/about and is very much a part of what we do.

Happiness does not need to be set aside as some emotional response to future achievement, you can work at being happy right now.

Instead of waiting for happiness to arrive through your eventual financial success, consider happiness as something you can control now, for you, your family and your clients. If we assume that to be true, then the question is not, 'How do you achieve happiness?' but 'How do you implement happiness?'

Implement happiness

Much research has concluded that certain activities can help to achieve happiness in our lives (Reference and Insight: www.happinessworks.com). Accepting this provides hope and can make you feel immediately happier. Imagine how you would feel if you could implement happiness.

Many words are associated with happiness, such as empowerment, control, self-esteem, fairness, challenge, purpose, meaning, relationships, achievement, autonomy and inspiration.

Happiness is the opposite of stress, so to aim at happiness is to eliminate stress. Happiness is not achieved just with yet more income but instead by doing well. Beyond having a roof over your head and having enough money to live the life you want, there remain three basic psychological principles (determinants) which must be satisfied for people to be happy. Happiness is about what you do, why you do it, and how you relate to other people in what you do. These psychological determinants are:

1 Having a connection with others
2 Having the freedom to be yourself
3 Having self-esteem by making a difference

A determinant is defined as a factor which decisively affects the nature or outcome of something.

Put simply, if you can connect with more people, have the freedom to be yourself and make a positive difference in the lives of others, then you are first determining happiness and thereby being active in all three determinant areas. You are implementing happiness.

Happy Determinant 1.
Connect With More People

*'Communication – the human connection –
is the key to personal and career success.'*
Paul J. Meyer
Businessman

The first of the three determinants is equally as important
as the other two but is probably the one that will make the

greatest difference in your life and the reason it should take top place on the Venn diagram.

In 1990 there were over 220,000 financial advisers in the UK, which reduced by 2015 to approximately 24,000. Face-to-face sales and advice has diminished by more than 90%. Over the same twenty-five year period, the UK population has increased from 55 million to 67 million.

So financial adviser numbers have reduced, the population has increased and people are living longer. There are more adults than ever before. In addition, there is a greater complexity of financial advice needs than there was in 1990. This huge reduction in financial adviser numbers in relation to the increase in the adult population means there are more adults eligible for financial advice for every one financial adviser than in 1990. The figures imply that if you had 100 clients in 1990, you could easily have 1200 today. This has become known as the 'advice gap.'

So, the good news is that there are twelve times more adult people for each financial adviser in the UK to connect with. Fill your boots!

However, with that opportunity, comes a constraint. Increased regulation, the need for higher qualifications and increasing lawsuit threats have put the new financial adviser on the back foot. Government policy is always poised to change, especially on tax relief and pension rules, which can also put a strain on the new financial adviser's ability to react quickly to client demands. Thus, the idea of expanding an advisers client bank, by too many, appears to be impossible. Taking on another adviser or staff to spread the load is not cheap and is a risk to a firm's own financial stability. Corners are all too easily cut when constraints are imposed.

Despite the obvious increase in potential clients, many financial advisers just don't have the capacity.

The answer to this constraint and ability issue is to embrace modern technology to do the work for you. It does exist and is a real time saver. Financial advisers who embrace the new way of processing business make a substantial dent in their time constrained week.

Further, with such time saving, the happy financial adviser uses social media methodology to engage with a greater number of potential clients. One simple example is to have a happy client recommend you on a social media channel, such as Facebook.

In fact, connecting with more people has never been so easy and remember, every person is a potential client. But it is important to ensure you first have the capacity for new clients.

Improve your profile

Connecting with more clients starts with developing your personal profile.

I was once told, and now believe it, that if your picture does not show on Google search images, then you do not exist.

I was born in 1964, the last year of the baby boomers. The millennium child was born when technology growth exerted its influence on society. Today's children have been born with the smartphone being as natural to them as a TV was to me, and they no longer question how it works.

The fastest growing users of smart technology are the over fifties. They are the grandparents of the current youth and understand that to communicate with their grandchildren, they have to embrace technology.

These over-50s (the probable average age of your client base) are building their technology knowledge every day. They are online so much, that online is becoming standard. Your business is now expected to support and service its clients online.

When people engage with you, be they existing clients, new clients or just potential clients, they will want to know more about you. So they will Google you, check you out and compare feedback. They expect you to exist online. If you don't have an online profile, then you don't exist, and you will immediately lose credibility.

Maintaining client interaction online is important and keeping your online profile up to date is vital to your perceived credibility as a financial adviser– what you are seen to be doing and what others say about you is what matters. You need testimonials, feedback, recommendations, ratings, pictures, blogs, news content, guidance and advice examples. These are all 'assets' to your business and of greater value than any yellow pages adverts or local newspaper marketing.

The best way to connect with more people is to first connect online with your existing clients. Every client should have a login to value their investments, to provide projections to their pension savings, to access additional information and most importantly to know you are there looking after their best interests 24/7.

If you have this facility and just one client made a single recommendation about your service on their Facebook page, then their connections will see that recommendation. If one in ten of those connections 'like' the post, all of their connections will also 'like' it. If one in ten of those 'like' it, all of their connections will see it, and so on.

So get a profile, get your clients to use their online client web portal and get your clients to recommend your service. If your technology does not provide clients with a good enough online service for valuations, projections and the ability to save more, then consider a change.

Focused website

You don't need a ridiculously expensive internet site, but it must be up to date and interactive. Your clients should be able to follow the progress of their savings and investments against their given target, and this is best achieved through a client 'web portal.' Online provision is the usual these days, and in five years time, there will be very few paper valuations issued.

While many investment platforms provide online access, users are quite often taken away from your own web page to achieve this. Equally, why have a selection of logins for a variety of providers when one single client web portal could provide a valuation for many vendors – a web page that has a client login, which provides a direct connection with you and your client's investments.

Give your clients the ability to log in twenty-four hours a day to obtain current valuations. Although it is actually self-service, it is expected and should be part of your ongoing client support facility.

Always be pitching

In addition to your online profile, you need to improve your social (and business) pitch in order to attract prospective client interest. You should never be off duty – always be ready to pitch for your next clients, regardless of whether the circumstances of your meeting are social or business.

If you ask a financial adviser what they do, they will invariably answer, "I am a financial adviser" or the shorter version, "I am an IFA." It's a dull answer and 99% of the time will kill the conversation and the opportunity to bag a new client.

When new financial advisers attend our induction course, I love to ask them what they do for a living. I have yet to hear an engaging reply!

Your pitch is your moment to capture an audience, to capture intrigue and to prompt other questions. The title of what you do is irrelevant. More relevant is what you achieve for your clients. Pitching is essential to attracting more new clients. If you get the opportunity to speak to a potential new client, take it as an opportunity to pitch. Further, if you want to become more productive and to connect with more people, then you need to pitch effectively. It's that simple.

When and what to pitch?

Firstly, pitching takes imagination, effort, and practice. There is no short cut or magic potion. However, there is a process that works providing you stick to the right order. As a financial adviser there are two areas where you might find yourself needing to pitch:

- Social Pitch – this is generally short and explains who you are and what you do.
- Prospect Pitch – this is your Social Pitch expanded when you are prompted to do so by your listener. It is your full pitch, which you must be ready to deliver when an opportunity exists to acquire a new client.

Whether you are pitching to an audience, introducers, or potential new clients, your pitch should consist of five main points. Pitching is a straightforward and efficient way to introduce you, your experiences, the financial problems people face and, most importantly, your solution. When you know how best to pitch, you will be happier in life and in business. As a financial adviser it's one of your most powerful assets.

Your pitch process should work in order from one to five. In full flow it should take no longer than four minutes and could be as short as two minutes. The content depends on you and how you want to make it work, but it has to be engaging, enticing, enlightening, encouraging and emotional. So from here on in, practice your pitch. Do not provide your official job title as your answer, as if filling out a passport application, but instead provide a progressive answer, thus allowing your pitch to further engage your audience.

1 **Engage** – clarity and authority: Make sure you make it clear to your listener who you are and why you're worth listening to. You could state your experiences, explain your qualifications, cover any notable achievements or mention a respected friend who may have introduced you. It should be succinct.

2 **Entice** – explain the problems people face: If there's no problem, there's no business. However, as an experienced financial adviser you know there exists a savings gap, and that is a problem. Generally, people do not save enough or early enough. Equally, there exists an inheritance tax (IHT) gap. The wealthy do not gift enough or soon enough, and that too is a problem. In general, you could say there is an advice gap.Therefore, explain to your listener the reason you became a financial adviser. It is not because you thought you could make loads of money, it is because you want to, 'Change attitudes and help people to understand the importance of saving, investing and gifting.' You may add something like, 'You are good with your own money and realised you can use your knowledge to help others.'

3 **Enlighten** – explain your solution: Impart your advice strategy for solving these savings and gifting problems. Describe your process and methodology in providing solutions along with the benefits and outcomes. Educate your listener on your insight.

4 Encourage – offer your services: Have your audience understand what they should do to seek your advice and to bridge their own advice gap. Be clear about their next step and why. Financial advisers who end their pitch with a request for a no obligation meeting, connect with more clients. If you don't ask, you don't get.

5 Energise – drive their emotion: Don't finish on a flat note, instead end with a story about another client you successfully advised, where they were and where they are now. Generate their excitement and people will be encouraged by you. People can only remember so much first time, but they will certainly remember the way you left them feeling. Be sure to deliberately leave your prospects feeling confident.

Number 1 above, is your social pitch and the easiest to get right. It is all about engaging with your listener by clarifying who you are, what you do and providing authority to your subject. It is social as it is best used in a social environment when seeking business is not the purpose of the event you are attending. Here are some engaging 'social pitch' answers to the question, 'So, what do you do?'

1 If you work mostly with people who spend and save little, try this: 'I encourage people to think differently about their money.'

2 If you work mostly with people who want to invest, but their savings are insufficient, try this: 'I help people to build wealth by focusing on their asset shortfall.'

3 If you work mostly with people who are facing inheritance tax issues, try this: 'I specialise in working with wealthy clients to ensure they keep more of their money.'

Each of the above should engage you in a deeper conversation, typically inviting a positive response such as, 'Wow, I was not expecting that.' For each of those examples, you could expand as follows: *'Actually, I have twenty years experience in the financial services industry and currently work with over 200 clients both individuals and business overseeing assets under advice (AuA) of £12m'.*

Your social pitch can expand into your prospect pitch by moving into the next four stages. When pitching for new business, you need to first engage and only then entice your audience into further listening. Never miss the engage stage, by approaching common financial problems people face. A problem needs a solution, and your solution is for everyone to work with a financial adviser at the earliest opportunity. You should close this pitch by encouraging a no obligation consultation of their own personal financial position. Ensure your listener is left feeling confident. Say, for example, 'With the right plan in place, all my clients feel more confident about their financial future.' Give your clients every reason to want to feel the way your other clients do.

These examples are all based on the outcome you are trying to achieve and that result is for your clients to work with you in reaching a mutually agreed target. Their ultimate objective is to bridge the savings gap or to save their beneficiaries inheritance tax.

There is an advice gap, and a well-practiced pitch will help you to connect with more people and encourage them to take your advice. Practice makes perfect. Write down twenty pitches and test them in a mirror. Try them out at the next event you attend and review your attempts, then improve them. Eventually, you will have a pitch that will encourage conversation about what you do, why you do it and who will benefit.

Associations, groups, clubs and societies

To connect with more people, and therefore more clients, be sure to get out and about. Being visible in your community through taking part in society events, or by supporting local associations is a surefire way to build connections. The more connections you have, the greater your chance of generating new clients.

There is no point in having a great pitch if there is nobody to pitch to. Equally, there is no sense in having a great website or social media profile, if you are not visible.

Being part of a group, an association, society or club and more importantly, taking an active role in those groups, will enhance your life and make it more enjoyable. If you promote happiness and pitch your worth effectively, you will build your clients and your business.

The process of 'knowing your client' remains as good a phrase as any and that ethos can also work in reverse; know your adviser. There is no doubt that the best introductions to you and your services come directly from people who either know you or have done business with you.

There are local clubs and associations for every activity you do, and for those that you don't. There are the usual, golf club, country club and sports clubs or gym, a social club (and the pub). What about hobby clubs where you may acquire a useful skill. Don't forget the community associations and charities, who always welcome new people to help. Buying clubs are groups of people who collectively buy things to save money, some even invest and share ideas. Professional organisations run regular meetings, but most are through invitation and may involve a fee. The point is, if you want to connect with more people, and be happier, then you will benefit by being part of a club or association, and maybe, just maybe, you will enjoy yourself and gain a new client or two. There is a club for you to join somewhere.

KEY POINTS

Like the *Happy financial adviser*, you should...

- Ensure you connect with more people than just your family, close friends, and existing clients.
- Look to become a member of a local club and take part in a variety of other local associations, societies, and charities.
- Adopt an engaging social pitch and communication skill to ensure the people you meet have every encouragement to become your client.
- Generate many new clients, who may become your friends, and in turn, they introduce even more new clients to you, which will help you to build a strong long-term business.
- Blog regularly on your website with up to date, imaginative and current content.
- Have a strong and effective social media profile to drive traffic to your website and blogs, by posting url hyperlinks within the social media message (eg in a Tweet or FB post, etc.).
- Ask for your connections and clients to recommend you on social media which leads to even more new connections and more new business.

Happy Determinant 2.
Have The Freedom To Be Yourself

"May we think of freedom, not as the right to do as we please, but as the opportunity to do what is right."

Peter Marshall
Clergyman

People, including financial advisers, are happier when they have the freedom to express themselves. Having the freedom to be yourself is having the freedom to express your ideas and opinions through speech, writing, and other forms of communication but within the boundaries that would ordinarily cause harm.

Free your time

Having the freedom to be yourself is also about having the freedom of time as well as expression. To provide the time needed to focus on providing the right solutions for your clients, which are:

- That you offer impartial advice that is truly independent, unbiased and unrestricted
- That your advice is well documented, simple to understand and unique to them
- That you have their best interest at heart, at all times
- That you will help them and work with them to achieve their goals
- That you can provide quick online investment valuations and information
- That you are available when they need you most, for more advice and financial reassurance

To enable the above, you need to embrace new technology, which will give you time to build the right client relationships, where together you can focus on goals.

It is important that you have the freedom to be yourself, to control your own time, your own space, your own dress code (within the boundary of expectations) and educate your clients in the way you work – your client relationship should be a working partnership. Rather than having a client/adviser relationship in the traditional way, you should consider your relationship with your clients as a collaboration with the aim of achieving their personal financial ambitions. Their financial goals and targets should be a joint responsibility.

Today, technology means you no longer need an office base and can work from home. Broadband provides such freedoms. You can meet your clients in their home, in cafes, restaurants, hotel reception areas, motorway services and even at the golf course. Fewer advisers use an established office.

Client details can be easily recorded on tablets or on mobiles. Advisers can quickly record the meeting while fresh in the memory. Wi-Fi and mobile communication technologies have created a modern, flexible working environment. This is a benefit to financial advisers who chose to embrace it. There is no longer need to return to the office following a meeting to upload collected data. More time can be spent with clients allowing the discussion to flow more freely and focus on outcomes as well as the data details.

Technology is freedom, so I am amazed at how few financial advisers embrace it to help their business. Instead of engaging with the technology of freedom, they have instead become embroiled in the technology of complication. If technology is cheap it will be inadequate technology, familiar technology is outdated technology, and complex technology is unlikely to be simple! What is needed, is technology that matches your business structure and strategy and is simple, effective and unique.

Self-employed and independent (in life and advice)

Such freedom is essential for most financial advisers who are now recognising the necessity of being independent. When it comes to seeking new clients, having the freedom to offer financial advice on a broad range of financial products, to cover a wide range of needs, is essential. By interpretation, independence provides the freedom to offer clients unbiased and unrestricted financial advice and is hence a key part of being happy.

Consider employment. Employment can be restrictive in both time freedom and the way you work; traits usually established by your manager or employer. However, this is changing. Modern business practice recognises the need for flexible working and encourages input from employees, which leads to innovation. Empowerment is vital to happiness in the workplace as well as the importance of being challenged and feeling inspired. Equality and fairness are also positive attributes an employer should encourage.

Times are changing and so too are the traditional 'time-card' employment ideas. Flexible working hours, home at work incentives and even zero hours contracts are all in place to encourage empowerment and an element of employee/worker control.

Financial advisers are in an industry where clients interact directly with one adviser – it is unusual for a client to communicate with other advisers in a firm. It is a one-on-one relationship. In other words, if a financial adviser has a client, she or he has a business. When financial advisers move to another company, their clients move with them.

Some companies try to prevent this occurrence with strongly worded clauses in their contract of employment; a restrictive covenant. A restrictive covenant aims to prohibit an employee from competing with his ex-employer for a defined period of time after the employee has left the firm, or equally prevents the ex-employee from soliciting, communicating or dealing with their clients of the firm by using knowledge of those clients obtained directly through their employment. This can be defended by law.

However, an employer cannot prevent a client making the decision to use the services of an alternative financial adviser or firm. No matter how much of an objection is raised by an employer when a client cancels their services with the firm, they rarely regain that client.

Most self-employed financial advisers in the UK today, started out in an employed position and when they had built strong client confidence, in them, they simply went self-employed and their clients followed. Just like the pied piper of Hamlin, if the employer does not provide an excellent employment package for their employed financial advisers, the flute will come out.

Employed financial advisers are typically overworked, overmanaged and underpaid. Why bother, when all you need are a small number of clients to get you going, and to find some space, control, and freedom. Help is out there.

The traditional staid approach of being part of the employed financial industry, such as the traditions associated with merchant banking say, still exists today in some sectors, but this too is changing. In the UK, the historic term of 'merchant banker,' for example, refers to an adviser position in an investment bank. A place where you would see well-suited staff probably wearing black shoes, sharp pinstripe suits and where only a perfectly groomed image is acceptable. A spin off from the public school days that still influence some firms today.

Huge, highly furnished offices with established hierarchical traditions continue to be the benchmark in the financial industry, but again this is changing. Working from home is becoming routine and we will soon all be online, in the cloud and paid on results more than time. The millennial firms are changing the way we work, and it is no surprise that most are technology companies while few are established banking firms.

Uniform and dress code is another control, and while it conveys solidarity and collectiveness, being part of something, it is rarely a choice. I choose not to wear a tie. I find them uncomfortable, and that makes me unhappy, but I have the option. Equally, an article in the *Financial Times* recently headlined with 'The high heels dress code is stamped on'. It was reported that a female employee was sent home without pay for wearing the wrong shoes.

I understand that clients expect financial advisers to be smartly dressed and the Happy Financial Adviser will still wear a suit but only to express the message that she is serious about the job she does. She will display enough dress sense to build credibility but not so much that she overpowers the client.

There is a balance between expectation and having the freedom to present yourself in your own way, that is a major determinant of your happiness and your future financial success.

Your clients and new clients no longer expect the 'merchant banker' approach to financial services of a trussed dress code, but they do have some expectations which you must still express. Today's clients expect you to look smart but are more interested in what you can do for them.

Employee to self-employed to self-sufficiency

All too often, employed financial advisers who embark on the journey to self-employment are confused into thinking that the primary reason for self-employment is to just earn more money, which can cloud judgment when considering a suitable business model. For example, do financial advisers go the directly authorised (DA) route, join a network as an appointed representative (AR) or join an already established national organisation as a registered individual (RI)?

It is important to change this mostly misguided mindset of many advisers who are considering such a move from an employed position to a self-employed position. It is not exhaustive, but it will focus their transition based on three principles that they would otherwise not consider.

Change your way of life

The real reason to go self-employed is to change your way of life, from being reactive to your employer's demands and their restrictive controls, to a life of having more freedom to control your own time. This means becoming self-sufficient; and in control of your life, without the need to rely on others – a happier life of your choosing.

Most employed financial advisers have earned between £25,000 and £45,000 for many years, usually with a car allowance, office space provided, telephone costs paid and four weeks holiday per annum. Maybe even a pension contribution and other such added value benefits. They have managed to live on this income and allowances for many years without financial hardship. Their income as a percentage – typically less than 35% – of their given annual target. This begs the question, that when an adviser moves to self-employment why does he/she suddenly need (or expect) more money than their current salary? After all, they have been satisfied with this level of income for years.

There is no doubt that one aim is to earn more money, but this objective should be exactly that, an aim and not an immediate expectation. Don't be drawn into expecting high levels of income in your first two years of being self-employed. Those that do earn higher income immediately will bathe in a false degree of achievement – remember the house of cards; quick to build yet easily blown away! You should plan to create a *sustainable* high level of income and to do so you should first become 100% self-sufficient at a much lower level of revenue.

Principle 1: Be self-sufficient

Self-employment is about being 100% self-sufficient. This is your primary focus and the first measure of your success. It should be the first item in your mind's goal and the first aim you put into your business plan; a primary reason to leave employment. Being self-sufficient means, you are in control of your time, your own earning potential and hence your own destiny. Only when you have achieved self-sufficiency, can you then build your wealth.

Employment can be viewed as a life of dependency on others while self-employment is seen as a life of being independent. Self-sufficiency is a life of being truly independent. To achieve this, you must not restrict your opportunities and ensure you work from a centre of influence that has no bounds. By becoming an independent financial adviser, rather than the modern (prescribed) status of being a restricted adviser, you will develop the skills for long-term self-sufficiency and hence be truly independent.

Consider this. If your switch to self-employment hinges around third party promises of client contacts that will yield the income you feel you need, but such promises turn out to be nothing more than an erroneous notion, then your whole business will fail. If you rely on others for client introductions, then you are not self-sufficient. You are not in control of your own destiny. The only way to be self-sufficient is to be proactive in seeking your own contacts and in doing so, to manage your initial expectations.

Principle 2: Be proactive with your time

It is important to plan your first few weeks into self-employment and to contact as many people as you can to build your client list. Everyone you know, and everyone you don't yet know is a potential client. Your valuable time should be spent on contacting everyone you know to obtain a meeting and to explain the move you have made to self–employment. This is your first step to being self-sufficient.

You are taking a step from employed to self-employed and as with any business this should be a time of self-commitment. Your current income and lifestyle will suddenly change. You will have more time than you ever expected, yet no salary.

Time – use it wisely, do not waste it

Put your time into your business. While you were employed, you would be expected to be at work for at least 35 hours per week. Imagine the contacts you could build if you focused on reaching people for 35 hours. A typical telephonist at a UK call centre will make 200 calls per day. When was the last time you made 20 calls in a single week? Be proactive and not reactive. Find your own clients and contact them. I am not suggesting you spend hours cold calling, but if you have a list of customers then contact them. Consider other methods of meeting people that do not involve others or financial outlay. For example, join a local business society or consider presenting a topic at a local institute's event. These are all suitable and proactive ways of finding clients.

Principle 3: Manage your financial expectations

Lower your income expectations and save your money. You are building a business, so ensure you share your plan of activities with your family and ensure they understand that you will need to make financial sacrifices initially until you are fully self-sufficient. Your family will appreciate the involvement and support your transition.

Money – use it wisely, do not waste it

Holidays have to stop. Unnecessary spending has to stop. Before you spend, ask yourself this, 'Do I need it?' This may sound harsh, but you are embarking on a journey of self-sufficiency, and any unnecessary spending may jeopardise that transition. Expect to earn less than your employment income in the first year; you will reap the rewards later on. It is important to maintain an efficient business model that covers all aspects of business and not just a flat focus on base costs. Do not spend on items that are not important.

Being employed or self-employed is simply a status of tax. As an employee, you are subject to PAYE whereas a self-employed individual declares his/her tax annually.

The taxman is not interested in whether you can sustain a life of self-employment or not.

The point is that it is not self-employment you are seeking to achieve – it is sustainable self-sufficiency, and that has to be your primary goal. It does not happen overnight, and it is not reliant on others. It is not necessarily dependent upon your business partner, your commission/fee splits, your office space or the car you drive. While these are all factors of activity, becoming self-sufficient will remain a direct correlation to the effort and sacrifices you will need to make to achieve your own goals and to be responsible for your own destiny.

Contracts for services

Many people will view being self-employed as having the freedom to be yourself. While this is true among many business types, it is not always the case for financial advisers due to the ever demanding controls of the regulator. It is not easy to be a financial adviser and at the same time run a directly authorised business.

Financial advisers who want more time to enjoy their life are best advised to stay away from direct regulation since the opposite is true. The responsibility of running your own financial advice firm is huge, often underestimated and often regretted.

To ensure you have the freedom of time, maybe to focus more on your clients or your family, yet to still be self-employed, then the answer is to engage in a 'contract for services' arrangement with a national firm.

An employee will find it tough to transfer to such a contract for services, but in contrast, those who are directly authorised always embrace the change with welcome relief. The employed are limited in how to conduct themselves, by their employer's way of working. They have targets to achieve, constraints on time and expected to be present and visible, strict holiday conditions and endless hours spent reporting to their boss. Freedom is about having the ability to take control and focus on what is wanted from a working life.

You should not have to work when you do not feel like it. You should not feel guilty for taking a day off work. You should not feel pressured to generate more business. You should not feel you are working for someone else.

The answer is to go self-employed. But before you dash off and do that, self-employed does not necessarily mean more money! It does, however, mean you will have more control of your lifestyle allowing you to develop a better working relationship with your clients which will eventually convert to more money.

By self-employed, I do not mean running your own business. The best solution is to take a 'contract for services' and work with someone else. While they run the business, you focus on your clients. Running a business is time-consuming and costly. It does not always offer freedom, but instead more responsibility.

You have a responsibility to your clients in this industry, so don't extend that to staff, office buildings, insurances, local business tax, employee law, and regulation. Leave that to someone else.

Contracts for services are a major contributor to all areas of working in the UK today. Hundreds of such contracts for services (self-employed contracts) exist in the car industry, the technology industry, the oil industry, the nuclear industry and of course in the financial services advice industry. However, like everything, some contracts are better than others.

Control your own destiny, not by being directly authorised, but by outsourcing the regulation, professional indemnity insurance, document creation, branding, website and marketing, agency, and provider relationships, post control, software needs and other business related elements of your role.

KEY POINTS

Like the Happy Financial Adviser, you should...

- Apply for a self-employed contract for services arrangement with a reputable national firm allowing you to manage your own diary, your working hours and your own targets
- Provide independent financial advice which broadens your client spectrum so maximising opportunities

- Determine your own dress code, within the boundary of client expectation and not be governed by an employer
- Embrace new technology to simplify processes and to reduce administration time
- Educate your clients on the benefits of using client web portals to enhance their experience and to save your own valuable time
- Have the freedom to spend more time with your family, your friends and just as important, your clients, to ensure stronger relationships, to know your clients better and to maximise client understanding and opportunity

Happy Determinant 3.
Make A Positive Difference
To The Lives Of Others

'Each one of us can make a difference.
Together we make change.'
Barbara Mikulski
Politician

Making a difference in people's lives is the third and most
important of the key happy determinants and something

you can start today. Your job as a financial adviser is to persuade people to act, thus making a truly positive difference in their financial lives.

This determinant concludes the trio needed to ensure you are on track to achieve an immediate happiness to your life. The happy financial adviser talks about making a difference in peoples lives because she/he is best placed to do it.

Research by Mintel (2010) shows that from a survey of 2000 people more than 40% said they experience some kind of money worry. The same survey revealed that one in five admits to turning to drink when stressed, while more than one in ten light up a cigarette.

The top five concerns were money (40%), problems with friends and family members (25%), health (24%), stress at work (22%) and job security (21%).

The Happy Financial Adviser does not have to charge for simple monetary guidance. To encourage prospective clients to think about reducing outgoings and to consider saving instead is dinner party talk, but essential to the dismissive client who would rather spend what they earn. That guidance, as simple as it sounds, is very effective and a loss leader in business. It allows time to build a relationship with a future client. It is making a difference. It is saying to people that they have an alternative to spending to feel good; saving provides much greater fulfilment. Feeling good from spending is usually short term;

feeling happy because you have savings and value time, family and friends instead of things is a feeling that lasts and lasts. It is making a long-term positive difference.

Why use an adviser?

You know, as a financial adviser, that sometimes a client with some knowledge can be a dangerous thing. Do clients really know that what they want is actually what is right for them?

One question that clients may be asking is, 'Do I need financial advice at all?'

The short answer is an overwhelming, 'Yes'. The long answer is, that the financial advice industry is incredibly insular in its approach to development and progressive thinking, quite often reacting to ideas created by the regulator or government policy rather than clients or financial adviser demands. The way financial advice is delivered is not a real market and has a forced structure invented by bureaucrats. The best way to demonstrate the importance of financial advice and why it makes a difference, is to use an analogy.

An (advice) analogy

Consider an owner of a large house and vast garden who spends all his summer days cutting grass. He is the mower of a lawn, a lawn mower and with such a large lawn to mow he struggles. His lawn is huge, and it takes four hours solid to cut the grass, and he has had enough. He needs this time for himself, so he decides to hire someone to take on this onerous task for him.

Searching online, he comes across an advert 'Garden Managers', and so he phones the firm to enquire. Following a short conversation, he hires the chap to come twice a week through the summer months to cut his lawn and is charged £40 per week. All seems fine and entirely because the owner has got what he wanted – someone to cut his lawn. However, has he thought long term?

Similarly, his neighbour, who has the same size of lawn, is considering the same solution and also searches online for a person to cut his lawn. He was unaware that his neighbour had the same idea. However, on his search, he came across 'Truly Independent Gardeners.' Upon calling this firm, the gardener explains that he does cut lawns but that his business is primarily landscaping and he would like to see the garden and lawn in question to provide a good price.

When Truly Independent Gardeners arrive, they take a quick stroll around the garden and make a few notes before asking the owner a few questions about the shrubs, trees, lawn and importantly the line the sun takes around the garden. The owner wondered why he is so inquisitive since he just wanted the lawn cut and the gardener replies, 'I have noticed that the trees you have are covering the lawn and in autumn the lawn will be covered in leaves. This leads to wet conditions and eventually a very mossy lawn. I also notice that your shrubs are not flowering as they should be and this is because their general positions are not right for them; some need shade and others need sun. When we spoke, you also stated you were fed up with cutting such a large lawn, which to me, is a statement that you need a smaller lawn and not a person to mow it. We could cut your lawn at just £40 per week for thirty weeks of the year, but over five years that is £6,000. I am going to suggest we instead landscape the whole garden for you. We will reduce the lawn to a size you can manage and hence will enjoy again, well away from the trees, move the shrubs to gain the best of conditions for growth, health and summer flowers and in addition build some other features of our design. We can do all this for £4,000 and the result will be more beneficial to you not just now but in the long term – well into your retirement. Think of the increased value of your whole property if or when you come to sell. Before you make a decision, please give me just a few days to present you with a complete solution. Will you give us the time to do that?"

Impressed by the Gardeners knowledge and experience, he agrees to give the chap three days to draw a proposed landscape garden. Later that month, the work to do is accepted and implemented to the satisfaction of the owner.

Five years go by and neighbour 1 is still getting his lawn cut, but it is now £70 per week and so far he has spent over £6,000. He is about to retire and is no longer sure if he can continue with the payment, so is now considering selling the whole damn lot! He failed to plan for his future, preferring instead a short-term solution that has cost him in the long term. Short-term fixes are just that, short-term.

Neighbour 2 however, took the advice of Truly Independent Gardeners and had his whole garden landscaped. The result is delightful, and he now enjoys mowing his much smaller lawn which takes just twenty minutes before resting under his trees in the shade from the sun and enjoying the full and exquisite flowering of his shrubs and planters. He is often complimented on his garden by passers-by which pleases him. Today, unlike his neighbour, he has no need or desire to sell even though his property has increased in value.

In summary, Neighbour 1 got what he wanted and what he thought he needed, while Neighbour 2 took independent advice and is much better for it. The message is, Truly Independent Gardeners have made a positive and long-term difference to their client by promoting a business of advice instead of the taking of instruction. They do not take direction because it is not always the right solution for the client, no matter how much the client thinks it is.

Self-investment

There is a strong trend and encouragement from the general marketplace, for the general public, to make their own investment and pension provisions. You can search online for a suitable individual savings account (ISA) and within just a few clicks can invest £1,000s into the market. Most of these simple ISA investments are promoted by companies with familiar household names. They offer a straightforward, easy and cost effective way of investing or saving. It can take no longer than twenty minutes to complete an online form and invest. To protect the self-investor, there is the usual cancellation period.

This all sounds fantastic. However, such self-investment is deemed to be 'non-advised' and as such is not covered under professional indemnity insurance for financial advice. Should the investment turn out to be a poor idea, then your self-investors will have only themselves to blame and are therefore agreeing to self-liability.

It is also typical these days, for online buyers of any consumer product not to thoroughly read the terms and conditions of the transaction. People naturally trust the firms they buy from and tick the terms and conditions (T&C) box without so much as a glance at the, usually lengthy, document. Occasionally they will start to read the T&C but abandon the idea when presented with 500 words. Again, it is easy to dismiss the text because, 'It should be okay.' The point to realise is the lack of professional indemnity insurance on these self-invest contracts.

By ticking the box, the investor is taking full responsibility. Any negligence is all theirs!

In contrast, by providing advice, the financial adviser is already making a difference to their client by being fully regulated and having professional indemnity insurance to protect them.

The benefits of asset accumulation

Most financial advisers today have come from an industry that started in product sales and that background is hard to extinguish; it's natural to sell a product.

Most people who avoid seeking financial advice do so for one or more of these five reasons:

- There is no obvious benefit
- The cost of advice and affordability
- The time involved
- Past experiences of their family and friends
- The negative opinion of others
- Financial advisers are sales people

To make a positive difference in people's lives is to ensure they know that 'asset accumulation' to produce income is their primary goal. This income is needed to replace their employed income at some future time.

For example, plumbers are required to stop leaks, to improve the water supply to your bathroom, to resolve drainage issues. In fixing these problems they do not discuss the tools of their trade, they only fix the problem. Surgeons don't talk about their tools, they talk about the health issue and the outcome following surgery. They do not speak of forceps, clamps, occluders, retractors, distractors, positioners and stereotactic devices. Some of these tools you will never have heard of, and that is the point. Clients have needs, and financial advisers should focus on mending those needs with outcomes. The surgical instruments are all tools of surgeons and equally products and policies are tools of financial advisers. You should not talk to clients about the tools of your trade – the products and policies are used to solve a need.

There is no longer need to discuss products such as personal pensions or individual savings accounts as these are tools to accumulate assets. Financial advisers need to stop talking to clients about financial products. It's too easy to try to gain credibility by speaking to clients about ISA rules or pension freedoms, limits, and restrictions, or what is and is not allowed. Instead, set aside the product discussion and talk about what really matters; are they saving enough?

Targeting problems and goal setting is essential in making a positive difference, and the Happy Financial Adviser focuses on just two issues:

1 His/her client does not have enough assets to retire (the insufficient) or
2 Her/his client has more assets than needed (the sufficient)

Only when this is established can a solution be discussed. One has the need to save, the other has a need to gift. Keeping this simple differentiation will encourage your clients to seek solutions and with your help and advice, allow them to start to plan. If you can get this important message to your clients, it is a little win towards making a positive difference. The insufficient client will appreciate the simplicity of having a clear target and plan to achieve it. The sufficient client will understand the need to gift and start to plan for it. It's about making your clients aware of the big picture. How they save or how they gift is where the advice process starts and that's where your skills are required.

Practise what you preach

It is immoral to make a recommendation that you would not equally adopt for yourself. Make a difference in your own life and start to accumulate assets that can produce an income instead of buying things that only provide short-term gratification.

Quite often you come across professionals who help and advise people, but who ignore their own advice. This trait is all too typical in our industry. There are too many financial advisers who advise one way and then fail to act on their own advice.

While clients never seem to have saved enough, or cleared their mortgage, or are credit debt free, it is not untypical that their financial adviser has the same issues.

The general public has an image of a financial adviser as being wealthy. Surely, you might think, an expert in financial matters would drive an expensive car, live in a six bedroom house in a rich area and be always flying off to sunny climes. Maybe they should have a boat, the children would attend public school and they'd even own a second home in the country.

The opposite is surely ridiculous. You cannot have a financial adviser who is poor, who has made poor investment decisions, or failed to provide for their retirement. They must be wealthy since they know what to do. Surely?

Sadly this is not always the case. The image I painted above is not just an image the general public might expect, but one the financial adviser would equally expect. Yes, a sound financial adviser will make a good living, but that tends to translate into more spending. The image takes over, and high earnings are rarely saved.

My message is simple. As a financial adviser, it is vital to put your own savings and long-term investment plans in place before the spend, and more importantly, before you advise others.

One of the best questions a customer can put to you is, "Where do you put your money?"

Obviously, that should be irrelevant to the specifics of a client who may have very different circumstances. However the common goal for every client, who does not have excess wealth, is the need to build and accumulate assets. You need to accumulate assets and so do your less wealthy clients.

The downside of being good with money is the procrastination of savings. With greater income comes greater borrowing against that future income. The expensive car is leased, the grand house is heavily mortgaged, the public school fees are a monthly struggle and credit cards are high in debt.

Financial advisers who are able to display those various wealthy attributes appear to be very successful – but it may just be an image.

Customers or clients?

In financial services and financial advice speak, the consumer is known as 'a client'; one who engages with a professional for advice and assistance. I have a major issue with this terminology. Clients usually don't shop around whereas customers do. You want clients, not customers, so you have to ensure your customer becomes a client.

It may appear pedantic for a financial adviser to consider whether there is a difference between customers or clients, but there does exist a subtle difference in their perception of us and our value to them. To strengthen the difference, a client should be able to say, 'Having a financial adviser has made a difference in my life, for the better,' whereas a customer would see their financial adviser as their last adviser, someone they see only when they need help. How your clients see you, is a real test of your impact. A customer could say, 'I made an investment with a financial adviser a few years ago, and I think it's doing okay.'

Understanding if your client's life is better having taken your advice is not an easy task and only tends to be considered in hindsight. However, the best way to measure this is to set a target or goal and monitor progress towards that target annually. If a client has a £300,000 shortfall, say, in their retirement target and has given you £150,000 to invest over the next ten years to achieve that goal, then taking a high risk could be considered. However, best is to recognise that chance aside, doubling investment in ten years (72 rule) is a challenge and what is needed is more client funds to invest. The solution would be an agreed obligation to both the client and adviser to achieve the

£300,000 target together. The adviser will do what he/she can with the correctly assessed client risk, and the client will need to generate more money to invest from his or her remuneration. Such a relationship will cement your customer as a client to achieve the target. Even a short term goal will cement a stronger client/adviser bond. Investment without a target is aimless, and your customer will remain so and be more easily poached by another financial adviser who makes greater (usually speculative) promises of fund performance.

I believe that everyone should have a financial adviser. For those people who do engage with a financial adviser, the alternative to not having an adviser is very rarely considered. It will help you if you ask potential clients these two short question – maybe even as part of your pitch. Do you have a financial adviser? Do you know your shortfall? Remember to express that not all advisers are the same, and you will start to build a confident perception of yourself and ensure that potential clients do not become reliant on pub recommendations or the speculative performance promises of your competitors. People should close their ears to others and prepare to pay for high-quality advice, just as they are happy to pay for other professionals.

> The realistic alternative
> to financial advice is:
> • Do nothing
> • Do it yourself.

The rule of 72

This rule of 72 is a simple mathematical formula used in finance as a shortcut to estimate the number of years required to double your money at a given annual rate of return (http://www.investopedia.com/terms/r/rateofreturn.asp). The rule states that you divide the rate, expressed as a percentage, into 72

For example, take an investment of £100,000. If this is invested over ten years with the aim of doubling to £200,000, then the investment should return 7.2% per year. Hence the rule is 72 = 7.2 x 10.

This rule is not restricted to just 7.2% and 10 years, it also applies in reverse. An investment could equally double if it achieved 10% in just 7.2 years.

It also works for other two number combinations that multiply together to make 72. For example, 8 x 9 = 72 and 6 x 12 = 72. In these two examples, the rule of 72 estimates that an investment would double as follows:

- A return of 8% per year over 9 years or 9% per year over 8 years
- A return of 6% per year over 12 years or 12% per year over 6 years.

Be sure to note that this is an estimate. The best use of this rule is in the discussion, which could be social as well as in a business environment. If someone has a shortfall of £400,000 to achieve a figure to retire, then if an investment return of 7.2% could be attained, an investment of £100,000 would need to double twice over twenty years to bridge the shortfall. The financial adviser just needs to half the target amount to find a need of £200,000 in ten years and a half again to find £100,000 in a further ten years. It's an estimator to build credibility and aid connection with potential new clients.

I hear your question, 'Where does 7.2% investment return come from?' The rule also applies (though less accurate) to 6% over 12 years i.e. 72 = 6 x 12. It hence follows that when Warren Buffett claims (Buffett Says | Bloomberg via The Simple Dollar) that you should expect a 6 to 7% annual return in the stock market over the long term, he is equally saying that for your investment to double it will take approximately 10 to 12 years. Buffett describes his analysis to that kind of expected annual return as follows:

'The economy, as measured by gross domestic product, can be expected to grow at an annual rate of about 3% over the long term, and inflation of 2% would push nominal GDP growth to 5%. Stocks will probably rise at about that rate and dividend payments will boost total returns to 6 to 7%.'

So, while the rule of 72 is not accurate, used appropriately, it is a useful tool to enable a financial adviser to express the need for early investment. It helps the adviser to illustrate tangibly the impact that time has on growth, that investment alone will not achieve a client's expectations, and that they also need to invest more!

KEY POINTS

Like the Happy Financial Adviser, you should...

- Promote the benefits of financial advice based on the accumulation of assets for income and not have discussions about products. Products and policies are tools of the trade
- Do as you preach, work hard to save regularly to accumulate your own assets
- Recognise that self-investment is prominent and is a developing activity, but promote the idea that it should be complementary to having a financial adviser
- Recognise there are two kinds of clients, the insufficient who needs to save and the sufficient who need to gift
- Know your client and set ambitious savings targets to help them achieve both short and long term goals
- Be prepared to live a moderate lifestyle until you or your business grows to the point of financial security
- Persuade people to take high-quality financial advice as the alternative is doing nothing or doing it yourself
- Use the 72 Rule to express the effect time has on growth

Barriers Are No Threat To Your Happiness

> 'Limitations tend to be illusions or self-created barriers.'

Steven Redhead
Author of *Life Is Simply a Game*

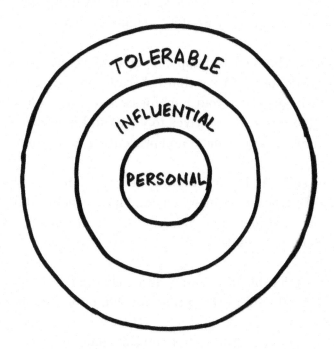

You now know that happiness can be achieved by implementing the three happy determinants into your working week.

As a financial adviser, you are already connecting with people but do you regularly see new clients? If you are self-employed, then you are working in an environment that provides you with some freedom but are you truly independent? You help people with their financial decisions, but are you really making a positive difference in their lives? If not, then you have barriers to ovecome.

However, you may have cynical thoughts about the concept of happiness and are still struggling to accept the findings despite the evidence. This is natural since happiness is used as a word to describe your emotional state and not normally used as a choice option.

You should choose to be happy. If you don't yet accept this as an option for you, then that is because you are bogged down with barriers to your happiness, and as a result, you are unable to see alternatives to your thinking. Barriers are clouding your judgment and preventing your progress.

In this section, I have highlighted the barriers that financial advisers face every day and have concluded that all obstacles, threats, and concerns can be categorised into three separate groups:

1   The tolerable (those you cannot change)
2   The influential (those that you can either accept or dismiss)
3   The personal (those that you can change)

By the end of this section, you will be able to analyse a perceived barrier or threat to your working day, your time or your ability to earn, and drop that barrier into a category. By knowing the three categories, you will know how best to react to that barrier, obstacle or threat, how to treat it and immunise yourself against it.

You will be able to see a barrier to your happiness exactly as it should be – no barrier at all. Instead, barriers will become nothing more than one of three processes you will be able to apply to allow you to move on positively.

Underneath the three barrier categories are a variety of barriers you already deal with. The point of this section is to ensure you have the tools in place to deal with threats and barriers that we don't yet know, but when they appear (and they will) you will be able to deal with them succinctly.

You will better understand the financial advice industry that you work in and how to overcome perceived barriers, threats, and constraints – those rules, regulations and constant changes, to which you must adhere.

I will outline the typical barriers to your progress in the financial services industry with the very positive message that it is essential to overcome these perceived barriers of business, life, and our changing industry.

You will learn to appreciate that the qualifications you hold to exist as a modern financial adviser don't automatically translate into a happy and fruitful career, but instead, your success is down to your own attitude in how you react to barriers and constraints. Being happy is a state of actuality and can be achieved today. Remaining happy is ensuring you overcome obstacles and barriers in pursuit of greater happiness and even bigger success.

You will have a better understanding of the right mindset to succeed in this industry and your role when compared to the pace of technological change.

With a better understanding of these barriers, and barrier categories, you will improve the way you think about the industry today and have a more positive outlook. You will be more appreciative of the role of the authorities in shaping the financial services profession to your benefit. In essence, you will understand the bigger picture and be in a position to briefly explain salient points about your industry to your clients, family, and friends. You will feel happier with every understanding and in turn start to appreciate that happiness is indeed a choice.

Barrier 1. The Tolerable

Government Policy, Regulation And Professional Indemnity

> *'Life would be tolerable but for its amusements.'*
> **George Bernard Shaw**
> Playwright

The UK financial advice market (the industry) is controlled by the policy makers, the regulators, and the insurance decision makers. We have little or no influence on their activities, rules or control. We simply have to tolerate what they say and do.

The best way to tolerate is to smile, take a deep breath and to 'get stuff done' (GSD). Sometimes, it is necessary to take a light hearted point of view – for example, the tolerable work on the basis of 'can do, can't do, and shouldn't do' and are best referred to as 'snap, crackle, and pop.' The Government make snap policy decisionswithout due regard to consequences; the regulator allows no time to implement change without the irritating crackle of yet more actions; and the friendly professional indemnity insurer pop and fizz when a complaint does actually manifest.

Constant regulatory meddling means you no longer have any control and instead you may feel no option but to move your business towards unwanted restricted models. Constant change undermines your very credibility and affects the trust that your client has in you. Constant policy interference causes confusion and invites fraud from the unscrupulous. Constant rule tampering quite often fails to protect and indeed only serves to increase client costs. Constant review interruption affects the very thing you are trying to achieve, and that is lifetime financial happiness for you and your clients; no wonder the financial advisers I meet on a regular basis feel so unhappy!

However, being unhappy with this group of threats and barriers is affecting performance and allowing misery to invade your world. You would rather get rid of regulation. But imagine the world without regulation or controls. Basically, it would be chaos. It would be worse. Maybe it is not regulation that is the problem?

When I was advising, I came across a compliance department that appeared not to help me in any way. I blamed them for putting barriers in front of my business. In a heated email, I sent a complaint to the then Managing Director (David Harrison) in an appeal to his better nature to intervene in what I perceived as unnecessary prevention. In his reply to me he posed the question, 'Andrew, have you considered that the issue might be you?' He was right. It was me. I had not managed to accept what had to be and failed to recognise that some things just need to be tolerated.

Over the last twenty years, it has been raining regulation with very little break between showers. Between 2010 and 2014 that rain intensified to a deluge that has changed the industry landscape significantly, washing away the dead wood; a mudslide to demolish the past and to take out the target driven managers and bank advisers.

We need to forget about the past and grasp the opportunity presented to us because of regulatory activity. Today's financial advisers are resilient and need to be opportunistic in this brave new world. Dwelling on better days gone by is pointless, as pointless as fans dwelling on Manchester United's football achievements under Sir Alex Ferguson; all that engenders is false expectation which can be damaging to progress.

The world is changing, and some are citing the end of global liberalism with a sharp return to the more DIY capitalist models. As a result, there will be a leadership, advice and guidance vacuum. In such a world, your success is in your hands – not in the hands of others. Your very happiness and your ultimate success are determined by how you react to threats and your behaviour towards those threats. You may not like it or even believe it, but you are in control of your future and the barriers you face.

There are those in the industry who would rather do without regulation and those, including me, who believe it is essential. The questions posed are:

1 How much regulation is too much?
2 Am I prepared to tolerate it and instead just get stuff done?

The Financial Conduct Authority

The Financial Conduct Authority or FCA regulates financial firms (including financial advice firms) that provide services to consumers. It exists to maintain the integrity of the UK's financial markets. Like its predecessor the FSA, the FCA is structured as a company limited by guarantee. Their website states:

> 'We want consumers to be able to trust that the firms we regulate have their best interests at heart by providing them with appropriate products and services. To achieve this, we have three objectives, set out for us in the Financial Services Act 2012:

- Protect consumers – We secure an appropriate degree of protection for consumers.
- Protect financial markets – We protect and enhance the integrity of the UK financial system.
- Promote competition – We promote effective competition in the interests of consumers.

There is no doubt that we should all approve of their claim to protect and encourage competition. Their three primary objectives are more than acceptable, and very few financial advisers would argue against their sentiment. However, there has been a steady drift towards 'over-protection' and 'under promotion' in such a way that the first and third of the stated objectives now contradict each other.

Regulated financial advice has become so weighted towards the consumer (client or customer) that their sense of personal responsibility or their own wisdom has been eradicated. If a client seeks advice, then the FCA would conclude that the adviser is responsible for every aspect of that advice and the client is in no way responsible. This approach does indeed satisfy the protection element to the FCA objectives, but at the same time, it begins to remove competition and instead, places the advice industry in reverse. By competition, they mean value for money or low-cost advice and cheap products. But why would an adviser charge less for advice if the potential for future liability falls 100% to them?

Any financial advice given must last forever with no time bar. 50% of all complaints are upheld by the Financial Ombudsman Service (FOS) so no wonder financial advisers, for whom there is little or no protection, have left the industry in droves. There is no 'long stop' time bar for a complaint, which puts pressure on the industry and costs, and high costs smother competition. There is a severe imbalance in the way the FCA focuses on consumer protection while doing little to promote serious competition.

The year on year meddling (with no doubt good intentions) of the regulator has forgotten to treat people with respect. If you were to believe the regulator, people are constantly in need of protection from unscrupulous financial advisers and never from the regulator's own (numerous) meddling decisions.

Ignoring the letter change from FSA (Financial Services Authority) to FCA (Financial Conduct Authority), this is the same regulator who thought it a good idea to invent the concept of 'restricted advice,' while at the same time insisting that all financial advisers should expand their knowledge through higher qualifications. When these higher qualifications were achieved, at great respect to the financial advisers for responding positively and getting on with it, the regulator dismantled the need for such excellent standards by allowing a restricted advice process! What was the point of expanding knowledge to offer a limited service?

Timeline of UK regulatory events and the advice process

To fully understand the FCA regulation, we must first look at the history of its construction.

The 1980s saw the introduction of the modern financial regulatory system, very different to what we see today. This decade introduced self-regulation for asset managers as well as statutory oversight for banks and insurers. The *Financial Services Act* in 1986 marks the start of a change that would affect the nature of the UK investment regulation. In particular, 1988 sees the introduction of a self-regulatory system that has investor protection at the core with the introduction of five Self-Regulatory Organisations (SRO) that are tasked to create, monitor and ensure enforcement of the rules. Overseen by the Securities and Investment Board (SIB), each newly introduced SRO covered five different areas of financial services to include:

1 Futures broking and dealing
2 Financial intermediation
3 Investment management
4 Life assurance broking and
5 Securities broking

Also, banks came under the authority of the Bank of England while insurers came under the Department of Trade and Industry.

During the 1990s, the SROs – in particular, the SRO representing the 'financial intermediation' – introduced principles of business applying to the conduct and financial standing of all financial services authorised persons.

Following a series of regulatory failings, such as the Maxwell pension fund scandal, and the failure of Barings Bank, there was a variety of SRO core rule changes and SRO mergers. More relevant to our financial advice industry, the EU *Investment Services Directive* imposed changes at the start of 1996 to include reporting requirements which cut across self-regulation. Following a political change in 1997, the Securities and Investment Board (SIB) became the Financial Service Authority (FSA) ushering in the end to self-regulation.

The then FSA (now FCA) had four statutory objectives supported by a set of principles of good regulation. The objectives were:

- Market confidence (maintaining confidence in the UK financial system).
- Public awareness (promoting public understanding of the financial system).
- Consumer protection (securing an appropriate degree of protection for consumers).
- Financial crime reduction (reducing the possibility of regulated businesses to be used for purposes connected with a financial crime).

The supervisory culture at the FSA was often characterised by a series of overarching approaches and themes, such as more principles-based regulation and treating customers fairly.

The FSA Handbook set out rules to which regulated firms are accountable and has become increasingly prescribed by EU legislation.

The FSA grew in size and cost through greater activity for the Financial Ombudsman Service (FOS) and increasing calls on the Financial Services Compensation Scheme (FSCS), fuelled by a growing number of consumer complaints especially around bank charges and payment protection insurance.

In 2012, the Government announced the planned breakup of the FSA. It transferred the prudential supervision of banks and insurers to the Prudential Regulatory Authority (PRA), a new subsidiary of the Bank of England, with clearing house monitoring to be undertaken directly by the Bank of England.

The FSA was renamed the Financial Conduct Authority (FCA), introducing more intrusive supervision. This was not just a letter change, alongside other changes, but a commitment to challenge a firm's own judgment concerning their business models, strategy and product development.

This is the regime we are governed by today. Having more intrusive supervision is the big swing that should finally separate the business of being an advisory firm from being an adviser. I firmly believe the two roles, although obviously related, are becoming mutually exclusive, certainly as an efficient business proposition. Like the toss of a coin, both heads and tails cannot be an outcome, unless the coins fall on its edge. In this analogy, that edge represents the unlikely balance needed to both advise and run a firm.

I predict that fewer financial advisers will be directly authorised and more will outsource their compliance and business aspects of their role to those who specialise in efficient, technologically advanced, IFA support. Currently, 91% of all Directly Authorised firms have fewer than six financial advisers. The costs and time associated with running a small firm and having to support a handful of financial advisers is not as profitable as it once was. Many such small firms are closing the door, de-risking their business and each going alone with the support of more specialist multi-adviser firms fit for the purpose.

When you consider the history, as briefly outlined above, there is a series of complex changes born from a combination of reaction to events and/or EU development in regulation. It's hard to dispute or dismiss the aims of the Regulator as anything but a drive for good practice.

Despite the moaning, good or bad, regulation is here to stay; we cannot change it without consensus and endless lobbying, so to get on with our business we have no choice but to tolerate it. But you still have a choice in how to better tolerate it. You can tolerate it directly yourself – or indirectly by working with those who will dilute the pain to bearable levels.

Professional indemnity insurance

It is a regulatory requirement for all financial adviser firms to have proper professional indemnity insurance. As well as it being a legal obligation, you need to fully understand what this insurance is, the relationship between insurer and firm, and why financial advice firms need it for their business. It is something we need and not just something to tolerate.

Professional indemnity insurance or PII is an insurance that protects financial advice firms against claims from dissatisfied clients. In the event of inappropriate advice leading to a financial loss for a client say, a firm may be subject to a claim which could damage the firm, and hence insurance is needed to protect the firm. This all makes sense. PII protects the firm and the claimant. However, the premium for such cover is huge and growing. Keeping the annual renewable premium low is a daily compliance challenge.

One of the single biggest threats to a directly authorised firm is the need to ensure, year on year that PII is obtainable. There is no guarantee. Firms that shut down, usually do so either because of high PII premiums or the failure to secure suitable insurance cover.

It is important to understand the difference between PII and public liability insurance. It has to be noted that PII does not cover any physical damage, which is covered separately by public liability. For example, if an injury should occur while visiting a firm of financial advisers this would be covered by public liability insurance. However, Professional indemnity insurance covers financial loss felt by clients as a direct result of the provision of a service or advice that is deemed to have been negligent.

If you had a home visit from a financial adviser and received advice, then you would be covered under the firm's professional indemnity insurance if that advice was deemed to be negligent in the future. What is important here is the distinct advantage of knowing your adviser has such PI insurance as opposed to not seeking advice and investing yourself. There is no cover if you get it wrong!

Negligence in financial advice terms can include many factors. Financial advice has to be suitable for the client at the time of the recommendation. The advice must be given after following a strictly regulated process of fact-finding, research, and presentation. This process should be recorded, and a full report or letter issued explaining the recommendation and how effecting this will benefit the client. The following main areas must be addressed:

- Client's attitude to risk
- Client's affordability and capacity for financial loss
- Client's age to retirement or other significant events
- Client's existing arrangements

- Cost of the recommendation and other financial disclosures

The knowledge that when clients take professional financial advice from you they are protected under PII should not be kept to yourself. Make sure your clients are fully aware of the protection they gain by engaging in your regulated services. Ensure your clients know that your business costs include the high fees associated with PII. It's an important factor when building your professional credibility, so make sure you cover this point when explaining your terms of business or initial disclosure document.

Equally, make it clear to your clients (or potential clients) that self-investing has no such protection. In other words, the cost of advice includes the cost of protection.

Government policy

It is important to remember that regulation is supported by the government and every time the government or the treasury make tax changes or product changes it has a tremendous impact on the people they serve. Quite often such rules changes are poorly thought out and need some further intervention. George Osborne introduced 'pension freedom' and has since left office. Those that are left to deal with such changes are those in the industry. They are the fund manager, regulator, compliance department, professional indemnity insurer, and investment or pension industry. It's about people's lives, and the very people that are supposed to be protected (the consumer) can be let down by poor government policy. While the regulator has poured everything behind consumer protection, there is little evidence that competition has been promoted or that government policy has added to that protection.

Despite every governmental or regulatory action, the general public remains indifferent. They are also further and further away from financial security than ever before, and the cost of financial advice has gone up. There is a well-recognised savings gap, and now, there is a growing advice gap. In fact, the warning is, 'Mind the gap.'

Mind the gap!

What actually matters in this industry are the people and the opportunities they have. We all need money to live. Money (for most) is provided through work. Work, as we understand it on a typical Monday morning commute, is the giving of time in exchange for money. If we did not need the money, we would not work. The success of the Lottery is a testament to that sentiment.

Deep down, although you (and your clients) probably buy a lottery ticket, you do so to gain quick money and therefore to avoid the struggle to earn it. However, you also probably know that after the immediate elation of a lottery win, when life settles back to normal, the winners are no happier. This is because they have missed the struggle to achieve the money in the first place and in doing so, missed out years of happiness. Happiness must come first.

I don't enter the lottery; I prefer the struggle!

The point is, irrespective of the Government policy, the FCA or the PII, it is up to you as the financial adviser to educate your clients on shortfall. To have them think about providing for the future and not just for today. To mind the gap and act with trustworthiness, diligence, and professionalism to:

- Ensure protection exists by doing a good job – experience, and qualifications
- Ensure there is cost effective Financial Advice – use of technology
- Ensure competition by the offering of choice – promote independence

Is compliance a benefit or burden?

The collective noun in our industry defining government policy, regulation and professional indemnity insurance is compliance. Compliance is the financial adviser's daily barrier – compulsory, controlling and costly in both time and money. But it has to be so, since the consequences of not abiding with compliant demands could be a swift exit from the industry.

Compliance teams are quite often blamed for their interventions when checking cases, or for the increase in documentation required to complete a case. However, every compliance directive is as a result of the higher burden placed on firms and their advisers.

The focus, therefore, has to be on being 100% compliant and accept that the greater burden being passed down is simply something you just have to get on with. You have to accept and tolerate the fact that compliance departments work in your best interest based on higher facts, meetings, and instruction from a combination of the regulator, the insurer, and government policy.

Focus on the benefit instead. Compliance is there to look after you, to ensure you are being protected and that you will leave the industry under your own steam and not under someone else's. Have you ever noticed that compliant and complaint are remarkably similar words? Further, make sure your client's know that you are being protected by having a compliance facility and process to follow, which is there to keep you – and therefore your clients – safe.

Turn compliance to your advantage. Make sure your clients know that it is for their ultimate benefit that your business is regularly checked to ensure you provide the highest standards.

KEY POINTS

Like the the *Happy Financial Adviser*, you should...

- Understand the historical timeline that has determined the growth in regulation and the development of processes, rules, and conduct to principles
- Recognise that policy changes, regulation and PII interference are here to stay
- Understand that a compliance function is to interpret regulatory demands and to lay out processes and procedures to protect the firm and the individual financial adviser from loss of position, money or both
- Appreciate that there is (currently) no maximum time limit for a complaint to be considered, which could impact long-term on your retirement
- Believe in the compliance process to also protect your client from accidental negligence or misinterpretation as a possible consequence of constant change
- Accept compliance as an essential part of offering a robust client proposition in a complicated business and just follow their judgment, as help, on every occasion
- Realise that strict regulation and RDR has reduced financial adviser numbers, leaving a potential client surplus known as the advice gap; an opportunity not to be missed
- View the regulatory barriers and threats as something to tolerate and manage or to be managed on your behalf

Barrier 2. The Influential

Broker Consultants, New Technology
And The Media

> *'It takes tremendous discipline to control the influence, the power you have over other people's lives.'*
> **Clint Eastwood**

Overcoming barriers is all about identifying what you can and cannot change. The last chapter was all about the barriers you must tolerate, they being government policy, regulation, and professional indemnity insurers. They are barriers that are in your way every day, but you must tolerate them to advance – it's called being compliant.

In contrast, this chapter is all about the barriers you cannot see. They creep up on you and can overwhelm your day. You can manage them, providing you engage on your terms and remain in control. These barriers are the 'influential barriers' and are optional. They usually arrive at your door without invitation. Their aim is to distract you from your daily routines, to infiltrate your confidence and to dilute your understanding of what you think you know. You can accept them or discard them as you see fit.

When it comes to compliance issues, by far the biggest cause of non-compliance is the influence brought about by media news, product providers and the business consultants who go to great lengths to promote their products or business support technology to you. Equally, financial advisers can easily choose the wrong business model for their lifestyle and the technology associated, just through the influence of the sales people.

To prevent influential barriers, especially from business consultants (and other sales people), you must stop outsourcing your own thought process, the most dangerous of which, is doing what others say just because it is simple, it appears to be a good idea or because it appears to be popular with others.

This is your life and your lifestyle business, not somebody else's, so make sure you learn before you earn and seek knowledge, understanding and careful consideration before embarking on someone else's pathway. In the end, it may be that the first proposal was right, but seeking out alternatives will not diminish your first choice but enhance the attraction.

Products and broker consultants

Historically, as already established, financial advisers were sales people of financial products. They were good at selling. However, they can also fall into the trap of being sold to.

Broker consultants are sales people with little regard for you unless you buy from them. They not only sell you the idea of 'a great product for your client,' but 'great software for your businesses.' I see the trap door opening every day. A financial adviser will feel they have had a good day if all day they researched some software, observed it in action on a webinar and signed for a trial period. Yet this activity has wasted time and money; it's probably something you don't' need or are unlikely to use.

Conversely, there is everything to gain from using a broker consultant as a support facility. When you have completed your background work in a need area for your business and instigated a meeting with a business consultant or representative, then you are in control. The rule is, don't be someone else's lackey! Don't become their indirect sales person or their foolish buyer of barely needed technology.

Equally, financial services products should not be discussed, promoted or considered, for a client, without first completing a consultation to identify needs and then following that up with proper research specific for the client. Only at that point would there be a requirement for a product to be considered, then promoted, then discussed. It is important to avoid the product discussion with clients, which clouds judgment and can only serve the provider and their representative.

Platforms and fund supermarkets

One area of development that has changed the way we advise clients combines technology and products, putting all your client's funds in one place which has the advantage of being easier to monitor value and performance. Traditionally, a client would expect to get a statement from their adviser or individual investment company twice a year, but with the development of fund supermarkets and now platform wrappers, this approach has changed the way product providers communicate with their investors. Buying funds through a supermarket means you and your clients can monitor them every day.

Unfortunately, some platforms and some financial advisers have made these platforms unnecessarily complicated. What most clients want are answers to two questions:

- Valuations – What is my investment worth today?
- Reassurance – Is my investment still right for me?

A platform that focuses on those two wants will provide the minimum cost to run the platform making it affordable and provide enough functionality that will last.

But just as most investors became accustomed to fund supermarkets, the investment industry started to use words like 'platform' and 'wrap,' confusing many clients (and some financial advisers). So how do these entities differ from a fund supermarket?

The distinctions are not clear-cut, which is possibly what confuses investors. In short, a fund supermarket can be called a platform and, on that platform, an investor can access wrappers such as ISAs (Individual Savings Accounts) and SIPPs (Self Invested Personal Pensions). So, a (tax) wrapper is a product, which has a choice of funds available, selected from the platform. The question that follows is, therefore, is a platform a product?

A simple way to remember which is which, is to consider a fund supermarket as being offered to investors directly, but platforms and wraps are terms used by financial advisers and are a reference to the method by which they manage investments on behalf of clients.

In fact, no less a body than the Financial Conduct Authority (FCA) has viewed platforms as online services used by intermediaries (and sometimes consumers directly) to see and manage their investment portfolios.

So, a platform is not considered as a product, regarding regulated products but the wraps that sit on the platforms are, such as ISA and SIPP. But it has to be pointed out to financial advisers that a platform is indeed a product suitable for your business support functions, just as other technology used in your office. It could be argued, therefore, that by restricting access to just one platform, you have restricted use of the product range under offer on that platform. By interpretation, an independent financial adviser would need to ensure all product types are available. But to be a truly independent business, a firm should make sure all platforms (although not products *per se*) should be accessible too, within the business support reason of functionality and usefulness.

Financial adviser or business people

I know many financial advisers, and few of them hold business qualifications. Equally, I know many business people and few are strong financially, they tend to rely on their accountants. The role of being both a financial adviser and a business person running a multi-adviser business is counter-intuitive.

It may be intuitive to think that if a person knows so much about personal or corporate finance that they would also know how to run a business. Even more intuitive would be the idea that an accountant would be a natural business person, yet again this is not always the case. I recently played golf with a young accountancy undergraduate who told me that very little business management is taught as part of his degree, which does not surprise me.

Over the last twenty years, financial advice has developed into a specialist area of personal and corporate support and equal to that of an accountant or solicitor. This trio of accountant, solicitor, and financial adviser have mutually independent skills, expertise and knowledge and together are a powerful combination to support any individual, SME (small- and medium-sized enterprise) or large corporate business. Every person will pay for services from at least one of those professions in their lifetime, if not all three, but it still does not mean they are good at running their own business.

Let's not get confused here. The activities associated with running a successful company, such as staff management, planning, leading, motivating, monitoring, organising, developing and training are not natural to the typical professional and more often, these required functions either get in the way or have to be learned as the business progresses in size.

With FCA regulation being so prominent in the financial advice business, a directly authorised firm will spend less time on client-facing and client-specific tasks and more time on existing in business.

Clients do not see the amount of background work needed to process a piece of advised business so as to satisfy compliance. Further, they see and understand even less of what a firm needs to do, just to exist. For example, a small firm of advisers that turns over £1m must hold £50,000 in reserves at all times.

Many financial advisers start their own directly authorised business, usually with another financial adviser. Their strategy may include expansion to recruit other financial advisers to their firm, yet little consideration is given to that complexity. A principal of a firm cannot both advise his clients and run a multi-adviser firm to any successful level, despite what many recruitment consultants may have them believe. As the number of advisers grows, time will be split between their own clients, the growing needs of their advisers, and their business. Stretched to breaking, the solution would be to recruit administration staff. This just simply extends the principal further and places tremendous strain on their efficiencies.

There is no doubt in my mind, that the greatest barrier to happiness and success is the attempt to both advise clients and build a multi-adviser business. This is an optional barrier influenced by the belief that it is possible, but you need to decide one direction or the other.

Financial advisers do not need to be businessmen or business women to have a great, happy and fruitful business providing they partner with a firm who are strong on the business side of the industry. Today, an adviser can work from home and spend every working hour of their choosing focused on their clients; in other words ensuring they are efficient in business.

Robo-advice

As previously mentioned, there are over 12 times more people per financial adviser who could benefit from financial advice today than 25years ago. There are only 24,000 financial advisers compared to the 220,000 in 1990. This is the crux of the so-called advice gap, which effectively means people are unlikely to make decent financial plans, make regular savings contributions, or bother with valuable financial protection. Equally, the government, having announced pension freedom (and then backtracking somewhat), doesn't want lots of people using their new found freedom to make errors of judgment or mistakes.

As indicated, 25 years ago there were plenty more people providing financial advice. Regulation is good, but it too has played a part in destroying that market and those that encouraged a generation to save something have been systematically removed. Very few firms now provide a direct sales force, and since 2008 the industry has seen a decline in financial advice availability at the high-street banks.

What has crept into the market on the back of the smart-phone technology boom is the idea of robots giving advice rather than humans. The so-called robo-advice business is a very real alternative to existing business models.

When all considered the robo-advice model is a real threat to the continued existence of the traditional face to face advice model. Since it's just software, there are no advisers, and all clients are owned by the company running the advice system. It's all technology, single platform, restricted product and aimed at providing clients with a quick, inexpensive solution to simple problems.

Robo-advice is described by the website, Investopedia, as:

> A robo-adviser is an online wealth management service that provides automated, algorithm-based portfolio management advice without the use of human financial planners. Robo-advisors (or robo-advisers) use the same software as traditional advisors, but usually only offer portfolio management and do not get involved in more personal aspects of wealth management, such as taxes and retirement or estate planning.

In other words, this is a restricted algorithm model that provides a limited solution to a limited problem by use of technology and is in no way personal. While robo-advice might have some place in the industry if will fail as a valid advice concept because it cannot replace the human subtlety needed to adjust recommendations according to both hard facts and soft facts – emotions. Emotions are the biggest single factor for any of us doing anything.

Robo-advice is no threat, and yet, the media would have you believe it is. It is an influential barrier we should consider and act on, but not worry about. You either choose to accept that robo-advice will replace you, you dismiss it or you act on it. I prefer the latter and so should you. Take comfort. As it says above, '...personal aspects of wealth management, such as taxes and retirement or estate planning' are not covered by robo-advice. While robo-advice might help reduce the savings gap, it is unlikely to reduce the advice gap for certain solutions which are best offered by specialist and impartial advisers.

The cost of advice has always been an issue, due to regulation and insurance needs. Financial advisers need to charge quite a lot just to stay in business. Robo-advice should be the solution to low-cost savings and investment by use of technology, but I fear that regulation will still play a big part, and the eventual cost will not be much cheaper than current face to face financial planning advice.

Investopedia also states:

> Robo-advisors are typically low-cost, have low account minimums, and attract younger investors who are more comfortable doing things online. The biggest difference is the distribution channel: previously, investors would have to go through a human, financial advisor to get the kind of portfolio management services robo-

advisors now offer, and those services would be bundled with additional services.

So, robo-advice is not human! Yet it is a human financial adviser that is sought 99 times out of 100. Robo-advice is the latest technology idea to overcome high levels of regulation, which tends to slow down the whole advice process, but the problem will always be with the questions, set by the programmers, which need an accurate answer to be able to progress to the next question. That's the point at which the client is referred to a human.

Robo-advice, therefore, will end up being less of an advice process and more of an introducer to a human financial adviser, or as I would prefer to call them – a proper financial adviser.

So, there is a real threat as this technology develops and of course as the marketing of such software takes a hold on typical customers. However, it should not take hold on clients, providing financial advisers introduce them to alternative technology first. I cannot remember the last time I watched a movie on a video let alone a DVD, it's natural to stream to any viewing device now. As with the film industry, various technology developments will challenge each other, and one will prevail above another on availability, cost, and functionality. For the financial adviser to survive the robo-advice threat, they just have to embrace the right business model, select the right supporting technology systems for their job and ensure their clients are introduced to a better and technologically advanced way of working that they have ever seen before.

Robo-advice is a real threat, not to the extent of replacing financial advisers, but to ensure today's new financial advisers make the right changes to survive and survive well. Robo-advice is an optional barrier. You either ignore it or accept it and hence make plans to beat it.

To stay ahead of such optional barriers, today's financial advisers will need to embrace the magic of modern technology and educate their clients with a better way of interacting with them through that technology, before the robot does!

Lifestyle cashflow modeling

This is best described as technology being half way between robo-advice and human advice. The data input will be similar to that of the robo-advice process but completed by the financial adviser on behalf of their client. The results will help the financial adviser to formulate their recommendation.

There is some way to go for these new software technologies to be exactly mid-way solutions, but in principle, they are the same fundamental calculators and algorithms. Most financial advisers have some access to cash flow modelling software, and it may help some advice cases, but it should not be a replacement for adviser intuition, knowledge and experience; it's just a tool.

Yet this kind of software is an example of another influential barrier that will cloud the judgment of thousands of financial advisers in the UK. This software, while useful, is not a need area. Use it if you like, but don't build your whole advice model around it. Don't be led by others and instead make your own judgment as to its use.

Cash flow modeling uses assumed rates of growth, income, tax, inflation, investment returns, lifestyle and spending. All combine to project future cash flow and such assumption combinations will compound on each other and ultimately be wrong. Regular financial adviser reviews are therefore essential, and reassessments of the cash flow are required to ensure the client remains on target. This is a negative for the adviser who is already stretched to maintain service standards for his existing clients. This means that such lengthy cash flow reviews will take up valuable time and maximise the number of clients he can service, effectively closing expansion to new business. It is therefore not the best use of technology, and there is a lot of the software that needs to be managed.

Consider this thought too. If there is a lot to be managed, there is a cost in time, and the eventual buyer of your business may not want to be burdened with that commitment.

The media

Your email inbox is littered with media news bulletins about your industry and the world around us.

It's nice to have information so readily available and being driven toward us, but be cautious. Media news is always followed by opinion and interpretation. Every opinion and every following action must be yours in the end. Be careful not to be drawn into an action you have not thoroughly considered.

Take the cash flow example above. A single article about the positives around Cash Flow modeling could end up diverting your planned day into cash flow research on the internet, followed by sales discussion, eventual webinar pitches to watch and a commitment to spend on this software. Something that you had no need for when you woke up, that you have now committed to purchase.

Although it may be a welcome distraction from routine, this is a deflection from what you should have been doing, without doubt making you a victim of another 'influential barrier' to your business. I am not saying do not engage with cash flow modeling. I am saying, make sure you are not 'outsourcing your thinking' to others and allowing influential barriers to cloud your business.

The media is responsible for truth and untruth, for fact and fiction, for important matters and also rubbish. They have to write something every day which is a huge demand on the young journalists trying to break into a better career position and all too often, we are dragged into that mire. Be careful with media hype.

KEY POINTS

Like the Happy Financial Adviser, you should...

- Easily identify when a barrier to business is influential and therefore optional, to either accept or decline
- Choose to be independent in thinking and not work for a product provider to sell their wares or in any way be a lackey to the broker consultant who aims to influence you for their own gain
- Understand the difference between a platform as a business tool and a platform wrap as a product
- Know that financial advice is your chosen business model best suited to your preferred lifestyle and not to exand into a multi-adviser business
- Recognise that the development of robo-advice business models are a threat to your business unless you embrace the magic of advanced technology with your clients
- Appreciate that additional software costs, such as cash flow modeling do not necessarily improve your advice process and in some circumstances could be counter efficient
- Not outsource your thinking when adopting new technology and in the end, use your own judgment

- Mistrust media news, opinion, and reporting unless real evidence reveals to the contrary

Barrier 3. The Personal
You, Your Advice And Your Credibility

> *'The gateways to wisdom and learning are always open, and more and more I am choosing to walk through them. Barriers, blocks, obstacles, and problems are personal teachers giving me the opportunity to move out of the past and into the Totality of Possibilities.'*
> **Louise L. Hay**
> Author

When things are going wrong, financial advisers tend to first blame others before themselves. This comes from either a lack of understanding of what is required or an ego that prevents self-investigation and an immature grip on the old ways of commission based sales preventing progress towards the new. Small and often insignificant matters of concern are blown up out of all proportion, always ignoring the bigger picture. Financial advisers have the best job in the world, yet made difficult when they refuse to adapt to new ideas.

Philosophically, you are the biggest barrier to your happiness and hence to your success. You need to be reasonable, wise or learned, calm and stoical, especially in the face of difficulties or disappointments.

You need to acquire energy, aspiration, and ambition. Create an earnest desire for some kind of achievement or distinction, honour, fame, or wealth, and the willingness to strive for its attainment. But in striving for this performance, you must ensure you enjoy the journey more than the eventual success, since success is the end point. Being happy in the struggle to achieve is better than waiting for happiness to follow your success.

You can overcome all barriers, the tolerable and the optional (influential), providing you can overcome your own negative inclinations. To make a positive difference in the lives of others, you first have to commit to that sentiment for yourself. In doing so, you will build confidence, which will enhance your ability to better advise and develop your credibility in the eyes of others, leading to greater connections. It is important that you understand and learn what you must do and when, and what you can do and when.

Ambition: a strong desire for success

When I was 26, I was working in the family business. I had been working there for nine years, since leaving school. Beyond O Levels I had no professional qualifications other than a heavy goods driving licence that I had never used.

I had fun in those nine years, just simply growing up, I suppose. I was married, had a baby boy and was living in the remote countryside of the Lake District.

I was making a decent living, had a car, a house (and mortgage) and was content. However, I was starting to wake up to the reality that 'this was it'. The family fruit and vegetable supply business was being slowly engulfed by the larger supermarkets. Garages started to provide food and other household consumables, and soon even they became our competition. Making a good profit became a problem. Hard work could keep us going, but maybe a significant change was a better solution.

The solution to many in West Cumbria was the same: if your business fails then you can always work at Sellafield, the nuclear power station that sits ominously on the nearby coastline. To many, that was a satisfactory outcome, but to me, I only saw a barrier to happiness. There was no way I was going to end up on that treadmill.

I had barriers. I had no decent qualifications, no professional skills other than the HGV driving licence and I didn't fancy forty years behind the wheel either. I had a wife and a young baby to support, and the business was failing. I made a decision.

I decided that I wanted to be employed in a large national company that offered prospects to management, access to working variety, maybe travel, enticing change and to experience a fruitful and fun working life. To achieve this, together with my wife, we sold up, shipped out and went to Edinburgh. I took a course of study that gave me entry to university and started a long journey that eventually led me to financial services.

I have kicked down so many barriers, my feet are sore! There are no barriers to happiness you cannot beat, except yourself. You are the biggest obstacle to your future happiness and hence your success.

The year I moved into financial services was 1995 – the time when FPC (Financial Planning Certificates) qualifications were introduced. Regulation happened and was perceived by many advisers at the time as a barrier to their future.

Barriers to our very existence appear almost weekly, and they can be insurmountable, but only if you let them. Work would be so dull without such obstacles and everyone would be able to do, what you do. Without a doubt, the most enjoyable times over the last 26 years have been the struggle. Easy is dull. The feeling and rewards from overcoming a challenge to achieve a successful outcome can be joyous but, looking back, I now realise that I should have enjoyed the journey more. Happiness should not be bound to success or achievement alone, it can be and should be with us at the start, middle and end of our working journey.

Financial advisers today have gone through tremendous change and in doing so have shown resilience, they deserve the results they desire. But they must not settle and prepare for yet another bout of huge change. This time it is not coming from our regulator directly, but from the modern demands of tomorrow's clients, the millennials and their successors. They expect everything from technology, which must simply work. Our challenge is to ensure we are ready for this 'all online' revolution and that we are capable of adapting accordingly. Otherwise our industry will continue to shrink.

The greatest barrier you have yet to face is of our own making – our children. Watch them, learn from them and seize the technology opportunity to your advantage. But remember, technology should only be used as a tool and never relied upon as an authority over human financial advice.

The retail distribution review (RDR) impact

The way financial advice is distributed in the UK has changed and will continue to change. The RDR was the biggest shake-up, ever, in the way advice is delivered in the UK.

Many financial advisers failed to reach the required qualifications to maintain their authorisation and of those who did reach the new eligibility levels, many decided not to continue and have since left the industry feeling unable to face the enduring administrative changes imposed.

Following RDR, the Financial Conduct Authority annual report (2013-2014) informed us that they have carried out some reviews into the way firms and individuals are meeting the requirements of RDR. Unsurprisingly, they indicated that they found significant failings in the disclosure of adviser charging models.

> FCA – "73% of firms failed to provide all the required information on the cost of advice and the scope of their service".

Let me put this statement another way. Only 27% (roughly one in four) have correctly embraced the imposed RDR changes. It is no wonder that when I meet financial advisers the length of the country from Glasgow to London, that they express their disengagement with the industry. Many have lost the ambition and motivation to continue as they once did. Many are concerned about their future and what the next regulatory meddling will bring. Many are fearful of the inevitable direction some supporting networks are taking them.

Change is the only constant

Financial advisers have been driven to adopt a fee-based business model (replacing commission) for pension and investment business, but to some, this has happened without the development of reason, and it is this failure to identify a cause for change that has left some individuals and firms struggling against the tide. If there is no obvious reason for change, then change does not easily happen. If change is evident to some and not to others, then there are errors in the delivery of change; leading some to a state of denial and abstinence.

> *'The chances are that you have already come to believe that happiness is unattainable. But men have attained it. And they have attained it by realising that happiness does not spring from the procuring of physical or mental pleasure but from the development of reason and the adjustment of conduct to principles.'*
> **Arnold Bennet**
> *How to Live on 24 Hours a Day*

The last of those words, '... the development of reason and the adjustment of conduct to principles" could not be more fitting to the post-RDR world of financial advice.

As I meet financial advisers across the UK, I see a lack of understanding, and I see very little happiness yet, with free thinking, happiness is still attainable. Consider this, if the above quote is broken down into the salient parts, it actually states:

- Happiness is achievable and others have attained it.
- Happiness does not just come from physical or mental pleasure
- Happiness comes from identifying a reason for change and adjusting to it.

Identify a reason for change

Therefore, to find happiness for financial advisers post-RDR, we have to find a reason (or at least invent one) to satisfy the question, 'Why change from commission to a fee-based model?' Forced change or otherwise, the reason for RDR was to improve the client experience of receiving advice, and this was set out by the then FSA (now FCA) in six outcomes:

1 Improved clarity of products and services
2 More consumers to have their needs and wants to be addressed
3 Improved standards of professionalism
4 Remuneration that allows competitive forces to work in favour of consumers
5 Viable firms able to deliver long term commitments

6 A regulatory framework that supports the above and does not inhibit future innovation

Surely no one can deny that the six outcomes for RDR are appealing to the consumer. These are the valid reasons for change and have been missed by many, post-RDR, or maybe just forgotten. The outcomes include words such as 'improved,' 'professionalism,' 'competitive forces,' 'commitments' and 'innovation'; all of which are very positive words to encourage positive outcomes.

It should encourage you to change, for the better, in the pursuit of happiness.

Charging fees

For pension and investment business there is no longer the ability to earn income via commission. You have to charge a fee for the advice you give and more importantly, for any ongoing service you provide.

When this idea was first mooted, it was a daunting proposition to the financial advice industry and many worried about how charging a fee for advice would ever be received by clients. They needn't have worried. As with many business transactions, the success is in the initial pitch. It's about good communication and delivery of your proposition.

While some financial advisers would welcome a return to the commission model, many have successfully transitioned to fee-based advice, and a return would put control back into the hands of the product providers. If anything good has come out of RDR, it's the more professional approach to business. It is the sharp distinction between the product provider and the intermediary, you.

Although the change from commission-based advice to fee-based advice has been a positive move, what has not changed that well is the transition of the mental process. The advice method used by advisers before RDR has hardly changed. Advisers are still led by providers and their products but not because of high commission returns, which was the original biased problem, but because the product fits and they know it. Advisers still sell products! Advisers still talk about 'top-ups,' or they process a product based upon the clients being 'insistent.' This is all nonsense and is a hangover from the days of commission. It is the one change that has dragged, and very few are dealing with it.

Your reason for change is to be happier – it's that simple! Stop fighting change and move with it. Take the journey – it's more fun. It has not been an easy transition, but one you would now not reverse.

Credibility

It is well documented that health and wealth are interrelated. For example, poor wealth can lead to poor health. While improvements are made to the delivery of better health and healthcare, there remain significant barriers to obtaining improved wealth. For most people it is the lack of three basic disciplines that leads to poor wealth underpinned by barriers and excuses:

1 Lack of knowledge – 'I don't understand' or 'It's too complicated.'
2 Lack of motivation – 'Why bother? We all die anyway.' or 'I don't earn enough to save.'
3 Lack of preservation – 'I just live for today' or 'Spend it, you can't take it with you.'

But instead of giving clients financial knowledge in how to build and preserve wealth, as the Money Advice Service aimed and failed to do, there is a very simple route that our regulators and we could take to better help and support the general public. Put simply, just as everyone should have a doctor for the benefit of health, everyone should have a financial adviser for the benefit of their wealth. This is a huge driver of mine, it's my big game. I want everyone to have access to an independent financial adviser, so promoting both credibility and low cost is important.

Having stated that, I should also qualify that I am no fan of using wealth, or wealth management as a term. It does not cover everyone and could put many potential clients off. Wealth as a word means 'an abundance of valuable possessions or money,' which is clearly not the case for everyone. It works in as much as, wealth goes well with health. However, they are terms related to an outcome or target. To be wealthy and healthy could be ambitions.

If you make the effort to identify and address your personal barriers, you will find change easy. When you do find that gear to make changes, do so in the direction of improving your credibility by being independent, approachable and affordable. You cannot demonstrate true credibility from in a restricted advice model.

The restricted financial adviser (FA)

People are different and have different goals and ambitions in life. When it comes to financial advice, why group your clients into a single category and restrict choice – surely they deserve a recommendation suitable to their actual needs, from the whole market. Don't they?

Financial advisers under a network are often assumed to lack the ability to make decisions or to make correct decisions. Therefore, many firms adopt the paternalistic stance of limiting the number or quality of recommendations their advisers may make. Advisers may be able to decide on the products, for example, but not on the overall choice or assessment of research for their clients. Yet, without practice in making decisions, advisers are maintained in long-term dependency relationships on their governing network of the firm. No one can become independent unless he or she is given the opportunity to make important decisions about his or her lifestyle.

Decision making shouldn't happen in a vacuum either. Decisions are best made when the individual adviser has sufficient information to weigh the possible consequences of various choices. Again, out of paternalism, many governing networks or financial adviser firms restrict such information, believing restriction to be in the adviser's (and hence their client's) best interest. This can become a self-fulfilling prophecy, since, lacking adequate information, advisers may make impulsive choices that confirm a network's beliefs in their inadequacy.

Having a range of options from which to make choices is vital to your credibility. Meaningful choice is not merely a matter of 'hamburgers or hot dogs?' or 'bowling or swimming?' If you prefer a salad or the library, you're out of luck!

Offering choice is a quality that rewards Independent advisers. On the other hand, choice for non-independent advisers is often labeled by disguise as 'restricted whole of market'. This is an example of how the word 'choice' results in positive qualities being redefined descriptively, but negatively; it's an oxymoron. Independence is being able to clearly state your broad offering and to stand up for choice, self-esteem and to make a positive difference in the lives of your clients by helping them to achieve the outcome he or she deserves.

Leaving your clients with the feeling of hope can make a difference and is an essential determinant in our happy determinant definition. A person who is hopeful believes in the possibility of future change and improvement; without hope, it can seem pointless to make an effort.

Accepting a restricted advice model is 'giving up' on your real role. It's a long-term personal barrier.

The independent financial adviser (IFA)

Traditionally, independent financial advisers were defined as being not tied to a single product provider or range of providers and therefore independent of such ties. They could advise clients on the most suitable product for their needs from a range of providers of their choice. They could also limit their range of advice.

Today, the independent financial adviser is one who has no restriction or limit on the range of retail products that they can advise on. By definition, they provide their clients with choice. In contrast, a restricted adviser is one who is not independent.

In reality, while they are unable to restrict their range of retail products, indeed having to consider all opportunities, they can limit the depth of providers across a single product type and usually only consider three at any time for comparison. Often, they use the same provider for a particular product type.

To further simplify matters, they tend to follow a due diligence process to identify a suitable investment platform to place pensions and investment. Independents can also use due diligence to operate an effectively restricted 'centralised investment proposition' as a pseudo-independent firm.

I recently met with a small two-man, directly authorised firm, who were looking to sell or merge with another firm. We were approached as a potential partner to their firm. They openly branded, registered and promoted themselves as being independent financial advisers. However, in conversation, they stated they don't offer Venture Capitalist Trust (VCT) as being too risky. This is pseudo-independence since they have a restricted choice. For the right person, a VCT offers significant tax advantages and not considering this as a matter of 'under rule' is false marketing to their clients.

In my mind, due diligence is a back door way of pre-selecting a product or provider for the benefit of the advising firm and not always best for the clients who's advice would follow.

While they can claim to be unrestricted, the idea of pre-selection through the process of due diligence does not make them unbiased.

The truly independent financial adviser (TIFA)

- Truly definition – 'with sincerity; without pretence; in accordance with truth or fact or reality.'
- Independent definition – 'free from external control and constraint: not controlled or influenced by a party or interested group.'

In general IFA terms, independent means the ability to recommend products from the whole of the market.

In additional terms, truly independent means the ability to recommend products from the whole of the market and to provide truly impartial advice without product provider influence or governance.

If a financial adviser is not tied to a product provider such as bank, life, pensions or investment company, they are usually known as an independent financial adviser (IFA for short). The independent title is one used by financial advisers to promote their impartiality. However, all too often this is not the case.

In contrast, a truly independent financial adviser (TIFA) treats every client individually, precisely matching product solutions to their client's own specific needs and not necessarily those having undergone due diligence.

Following years of marketing, today's clients still expect their financial adviser to be truly independent. Failing to be truly independent is failing to differentiate you from sales, or robo-advice, or being the lackey of some product provider or platform.

To be truly credible, you have to be truly independent.

Qualifications and skills

If you are a registered financial adviser in the UK today, you will have satisfied or met the QFC level 4 exam standards which is the framework most associated with vocational, or work-related qualifications.

You will have heard other industry people talking about qualification levels but not exactly sure of their accreditation. These levels are contained in three fundamental qualification frameworks:

- National Qualifications Framework (NQF)
- Qualifications and Credit Framework (QCF)
- Framework for Higher Education Qualifications (FHEQ)

The frameworks group together qualifications that place similar demands on you as a learner. However, within any one level, qualifications can cover a broad mix of subjects, and take different amounts of time to complete.

The Qualifications and Credit Framework (QCF) contains vocational (or work-related) qualifications, available in England, Wales and Northern Ireland.

These qualifications are made up of units that are worth credits. You can study units at your own pace and build these up to full qualifications of different sizes over time.

Expanding your knowledge is always positive, but fewer financial advisers are expanding their soft skills. Skills such as:

- Problem solving
- Adaptability
- Collaboration
- Strong work ethic
- Time management
- Critical thinking
- Self-confidence
- Handling pressure

Advancing their technology skills is also paramount in today's social-media-hungry world, it's where tomorrow's clients live. If you really want to make a difference in people's lives and benefit from the reward such difference will yield, then every financial adviser needs to expand their qualifications, soft skills and technology skills. Taking courses to acquire these skills is also connecting with others, one of the three happy determinants.

Failing to expand your skills is falling into the personal barrier trap which is a lack of self-development. It is your responsibility to change and develop your skills. To ensure you continue to improve and not just to sit on the already achieved qualifications as set out by the regulators.

Chartered Financial Planner will be the minimum bench mark in the future and many are working hard to achieve that qualification already. When more than 50% are chartered, a new minimum standard will be set.

To be happy, be healthy

I have already identified important personal barriers that you must overcome to ensure your future in business as a financial adviser is a happy one. However, there is an important link between your happiness in business and your personal health. The way you live your daily life is vital to your happiness and success in business.

There are daily choices which seem completely unrelated to your happiness in business, that significantly impact on your mental and physical well-being. At times we all eat too much, drink too much alcohol and slouch on the sofa. We don't get enough sleep, we don't take enough time out of work to enjoy life, and we don't spend sufficient time with family and friends. Little changes to improve your health are little wins towards a better, more effective working life.

Here are seven tips to ensure you change the way you live, on a daily basis, to improve your health and happiness. In reading these, see if you can identify which of the three happy determinants these seven represent; to connect with more people, have the freedom to be yourself and make a difference in the lives of others:

1 Seek meaningful connections (like marriage and staying in touch with family).

2 Get up, and get out. Just thirty minutes' walk every day will significantly improve your health.

3 Take a few moments to stop working and simply take a breath.

4 Become part of your local community and build lasting friendships.

5 Express yourself creatively. Solve your own problems and help others to solve theirs.

6 Contribute more and consume less – you will be healthier for it.

7 Work in a job you love and overcome personal barriers.

No single strategy will work for everyone, but the principles in this book offer you an alternative.

KEY POINTS

Like the Happy Financial Adviser, you should...

- Blame no-one for your errors, mishaps or blunders except yourself.
- Have a strong desire for financial success through happiness and be willing to change to achieve it.
- Recognise that change is the only real constant and always seeks self-improvement.

- Have the ability to identify that finding happiness is a reason for change and it can be achieved with increased effort.
- Ensure your credibility exists by promoting a truly independent advice process
- Understand your clients well and advise them uniquely and individually to their needs and not blanket them with the needs of others.
- Aim to improve skills beyond the standard of industry qualifications and self-development to include a broad range of skills.
- Welcome small changes and little wins as a move to improve and progress into a new financial advice world that will improve your health, build confidence and credibility.

SECTION C

Your Journey To Happiness

'The journey is what brings us happiness, not the destination.'

Dan Millman
Author

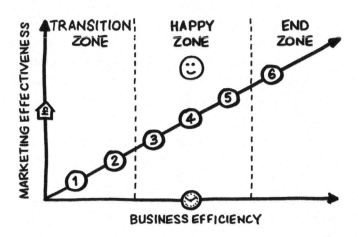

The first two sections of this book cover the three psychological determinants needed to be happier and the three groups of barriers you need to understand and overcome to ensure nothing gets in the way of your happiness.

In this section, I will take you through a six-step journey that I have created at Truly Independent Ltd to ensure those teachings can be applied in practice. Our structure, strategy, systems, services and support functions are the first five steps which empower our advisers to spend more time doing what they do best; being in front of their clients and providing their clients with a truly independent advice experience. The sixth and final step of your journey will be retirement preparation, or as we prefer to call it, succession.

Each six-step journey is designed to improve the way you work giving you more time and less stress. This valuable time is for you, to enjoy your own lifestyle or maybe for you to prospect for new clients making you more money if that is what you want. Either way, the outcome will be happiness for you, your family and your client.

These six steps can be grouped into three zones, as follows:

1 The Transition Zone: covering business structure and business strategy
2 The Happy Zone: covering issues around IT systems, client services, and adviser support
3 The Exit Zone: covering aspects of preparing for retirement

Each chapter in this section will deal with your choices as a financial adviser. I will cover the fundamentals of different financial advice models, what systems to use and how, how best to communicate your services to your clients and to charge the right fees. When and what support functions you and your clients will need now and in the future. I will explain your choices and by way of explanation, what Truly Independent Ltd have chosen to do, and why. Also, how our choices have impacted on our financial advisers and equally, why financial advisers from all advice models have decided to change career and join us.

This journey allows for all options available to you and will help you to make the decision for your chosen lifestyle. At the end of this section, you will know the right path for you.

Ultimately, I am sure you want to be happy and for both your family and clients to be happy too. To ensure that happiness, you must first ensure you are on the right journey.

Step 1. Structure

Define Your Financial Adviser
Business Model

> *'Definition, rationality, and structure are ways of seeing, but they become prisons when they blank out other ways of seeing.'*
>
> **A. R. Ammons**
> Poet

You cannot build anything strong without a strong foundation. Equally, you need to have the most appropriate structure worked out first, before you build. Arguably, you can only achieve more clarity and vision of your intended course, by first comparing alternatives.

The structure is not to be confused with strategy. The strategy is the business activity you will adopt, review and on occasions change as the industry changes around you. Strategy is the variable. In contrast, the structure is the stable framework and the stability element that defines your strategy. However, there are similarities and hence why I place both into the Transition Zone of my six-step journey.

Maybe you are an employed financial adviser considering a career change to being self-employed, or maybe you are already self-employed, in a network or a director/partner of a directly authorised firm, and have reached an impasse – whatever your position, if you are considering a change, you will need to define a new structure early on. Once established, a firm will find it difficult to change. While individuals can change, a firm is less flexible.

To consider a change, you need to identify the right business structure for you and in doing so answer three difficult questions each with two possible outcomes. Hence, mathematically leading to eight different business combinations.

1. Directly regulated or registered individual

All firms are regulated, but not all are directly regulated. Direct regulation means taking all guidance, rules, and instruction directly from the regulator, the FCA. In essence, being directly authorised (DA) is being 'on your own.'

It is important to point out at this stage that being a self-employed financial adviser means you have two roles to consider in your daily or weekly business:

- The non-client business activities
- The client-specific business activities

The non-client business activities are activities such as completing the yearly PII application form, or the six-monthly FCA report. It could be chasing fees from providers, reconciling commission/fee statements or dealing with agency issues. It could be supervision of other advisers or checking their cases. It could be updating your software or learning new software. It could be dealing with staff, office expenses, business rates, reordering stationery, updating your website or drafting newsletters. Hours could be spent reading endless compliance journals and regulatory directives. The point is, none of these activities will make you money because they are all non-client-specific. It is what being directly authorised is all about: administration, administration, administration.

In contrast, client-specific activities involve the client. It could be arranging a meeting or travelling to a meeting. It could be research activities following a client meeting or requesting valuations. It could be writing suitability letters or generating a quote. In fact, it is an activity that is unique to the client. It is client specific if the client either sees what you are preparing or will benefit from it at some point in the process. All these activities result in you being paid a fee and are productive activities.

If you just want to give client advice and build a focused client business, then being directly authorised is pointless. I know some two or three person firms that are directly authorised and they outsource some or all of their non-client-specific activities, but at what gain?

The message is simple, if you don't want non-client-specific activities or consider outsourcing these activities, then don't go directly authorised. If you only want to advise clients, then go registered individual with a reputable firm that is geared up to support you in that purpose.

Yes, you can buy external support from outside compliance companies, but they, being paid by you as their client, rarely criticise, which can be risky. File checks without valid criticism may give you a false impression of your real risk exposure.

It is worth mentioning early on, that outside compliance firms are rarely regulated and carry no liability if a complaint is ever upheld against a directly authorised financial adviser. In other words, they take no risk to their involvement or file check feedback, yet are still paid for it. What they may have, is reputation. However, when financial advisers tell me good things about an outsourced compliance firm who have checked their files, they usually mean the firm's controls have resulted in an acceptable level of feedback, with little action for the financial adviser.

To give you an example, if you take your car for a service and the garage reports no additional work needed, then you will be pleased because it usually means money and time is saved. However, does that mean the car is in excellent condition or that the garage has just covered the minimum number of tasks needed to complete the service? Only time will tell!

If you are considering the directly authorised route, just consider keeping your compliance internal – are you sure you want others packing your parachute!

Interestingly, a multi-adviser firm like Truly Independent Ltd means all the financial advisers are registered individuals (RI) of the firm and are sheltered from non-client-specific and mostly regulatory activities, yet each adviser will be effectively directly authorised.

There is a third alternative, (that you should know about but should not consider) that of being part of a network that is simply a further tier between the FCA and the registered individual. This tier is what is known as being an appointed representative (AR) of the network, but you will still be a registered individual of the appointed representative. This is a tier to be avoided. It offers similarities to being directly authorised such as your own brand, stationery, and agencies but without the full control. The risk is all yours. You usually pay fees, and firms who join such networks typically do so for low cost reasons. When financial advisers get in touch because they are considering joining us, I am very wary of those whose first questions involve, 'How much are you?' My experience of low cost is that it eventually breaks.

It follows, that if a model is based on low cost, then you will attract a host of financial advisers who need low cost just to continue in business. Cost should never be a primary reason to change. Similarly, the very principle of a network is to provide appointed representatives with their own brand, which unfortunately leads to the disparity of values across the whole network. Such disparity leads to inconsistency between the network firms (or individuals) and can only heighten risk. As a result, being part of a network involves working alongside other firms you know nothing about which can be unpredictable and unstable.

The DA model has more responsibility and administration than the other two models and with that greater control comes greater administration and accountability. In contrast, the RI model is less restrictive than the other two due to the lesser management burden and provide greater freedom to spend more time with client- specific business, which, in many cases is more profitable as a result.

Do not be misled by the word 'control' when it comes to highly-regulated financial services distribution in the UK. Control means choice but always at the cost of responsibility and the burden associated with non-client-specific administration. You cannot have more control without accepting more administration and risk.

It is my experience that the main two factors that have a direct effect on IFA production are the administration versus freedom – the more administration, the less time to see clients. It follows that less time with clients means less revenue for the business and quite often a sole trader RI will have the same net income as a sole trader DA due to the huge administration time associated with direct authorisation; consider the opportunity cost.

The AR model is the worst of all models. This is what the media says about AR Networks:

> "To be an appointed representative of a network was to be an employee in all but name, with all of the risks and none of the perks of owning your own business".
> (from Money Marketing – Do IFA networks have a future?.

Equally, it is worth noting the feeling of an adviser who said:

"I felt I was hanging in the breeze."
Quote from professional adviser – Ex-Financial Ltd speaks out.

On the face of it, the AR model sits between the other two models and appears to satisfy the 'best of both worlds' conditions, and that is the primary focus for Network recruiters. If that is true, then by sitting in the middle ground, it also satisfies the 'worst' of both worlds – a fact easily ignored because the AR model is sold as having control and usually low cost.

The only attraction is their low cost, they are generally cheap. It is the adviser's living so why buy cheap? Low-cost networks attract many advisers but this means low resources to adequately support the advisers.

Here are three reported examples where perceived control as an AR has ended in restructure and/or financial loss where control was effectively zero:

- Honister – 900 IFAs lost their AR business
- Financial Limited – closed to new recruitment for compliant irregularities
- Sesame – fined for irregular financial dealings with providers

2. Independent or restricted

I have already made a comment on the two regulated business models as defined by the FCA and now you need to make a choice as to which is best for you. Many firms are Restricted, many are Independent, but not all are *truly* independent. Clients expect their financial adviser to be independent because they understand it and are often sheltered from any alternative.

An Independent financial adviser (IFA) can only claim to be truly independent when they are 100% free from influential controls by product providers in areas or funding, ownership, high commissions and corporate hospitality.

Over the last twelve years, I have been involved in the recruitment, training and mentoring of independent financial advisers across the UK. The last six of those years I have recruited for my own company. The company was set up and developed with the client in mind, and this model continues to attract new advisers to join us every month, without any marketing. We have grown organically, have no debts, no liabilities and are not influenced by product providers.

I have witnessed every possible characteristic of financial advisers, the good, the bad and on one occasion the horrid. In this context, by horrid, I mean fraudulent! I have met the diligent, the grafter, the salesman, the academic, the lazy, the inexperienced, the egotistical, the untidy, the inefficient, the friendly, the hilarious, the angry, the wonderful, the blithering, the confused, the young, the old, the male and the female. I have met them all.

But the highly respected and Happy Financial Adviser stands out from the crowd. This person believes in providing financial advice to their clients that is truly independent. Their approach is to continually build an ever stronger client relationship. Some have achieved Chartered Financial Planner status but continue to attend courses on good practice to hone their consultation and questioning techniques. They have an excellent understanding of the industry with every focus on continuing self-development. They attend events in search of improvement. They are never short of new client introductions and have mastered their financial pitch in both their social circles not just business. They work diligently on their inefficiencies to reduce administrative burdens so creating valuable time for their clients and themselves. They know how to balance a work life relationship. They have financial success of their own and in developing their business the right way; they have a business ready for sale when they decide to retire. With good practice, they are highly regarded, have a great lifestyle and have financial security.

The restricted model exists typically to benefit a platform provider and financial advisers under this model can end up as an ISA sales person. While it has an active function to bridge the savings gap the restrictions limit the spread of advice needed to cover all aspects of financial planning.

It certainly goes against all aspects of chartered financial planning.

If you want cheap, go restricted. If you want easy, go restricted. If you want fast sales, go restricted. However, if you want happiness by connecting with more clients, by having the freedom to advise on any product and to make a difference in the lives of everyone you advise, then go independent. Being independent is the model of choice. Providing *truly* independent financial advice is what clients expect and what financial advisers would prefer to do.

Part of my job is to keep an eye on our competitors, and one way to do this is to read their websites. In doing so, I often read claims from independent financial adviser firms of their professional ability and value services to advise their clients – nothing wrong with that. Unusually, however, within that claim, there is typically a reference to being *truly* independent. Here are three examples of the phrases that I have taken straight from the websites of IFA's in the UK today:

'We are a truly independent organisation, free from the influence of any financial corporation. Our exclusive members represent the best in the UK, who, in turn, offer the highest standard of service.'

'At XYZ IFAs we are truly independent with no bias towards any one investment or provider.'

'We are truly independent and "whole of market"- not owned by a bank or insurance company so we are free to find the right solution for you.'

I am sure their advice is as they claim, truly independent. However, it is fascinating that each of the three firms listed above, like many more firms, feel the need to differentiate themselves from other IFAs who do not have the same claim.

By the FCA definition of restricted advice and independent advice, there is no mention of a third method, that of being *truly* Independent, yet many firms chose to define this as a distinct trait.

What is it about the need to claim to be truly independent?

The answer is surprisingly simple. It's the perception of the clients they (and we) are trying to attract. I recall a night out in Glasgow, and while chatting with friends, I overheard my friend talking to a woman at another table. When my friend was asked, 'So what do you do?' he replied, 'I am an independent financial adviser.' She then enquired, 'I see, but are you *truly* independent?' Well! I could not get my card out of my wallet fast enough.'He isn't, but I am!' I said.

The point is when it comes to brand, image and honesty, it is the general public that matter and they know more than you think (or than the regulator gives them credit for) about what it is to be truly independent.

In summary, clients expect you to be *truly* independent, and I don't blame any firm for claiming that niche, because many are not. But the decision is yours. If you want quick sales, simple products, and low cost then restricted could be for you.

3. Multi-adviser business or lifestyle business?

Do you have the enthusiasm and dedication to build and run a large multi-adviser business or is your focus more towards a social work/life balance?

There are only 24,000 Regulated financial advisers in the UK today. Twenty-five years ago there were ten times as many. Insurance sales people were speaking to their clients about saving, investing, pensions and protection on a daily basis. This was a time when a sale was the key driver and advice secondary.

Today all regulated financial advisers need to have a minimum of a Level 4 Diploma qualification in Regulated Financial Services (or equivalent), and they must abide by strict financial regulation. The swing from a fundamentally driven sales industry to an advice required industry could never be greater. While the result of change has been to the advantage of the client, with such vigorous change has come onerous regulation. There is time administrative demand on our financial advisers today. Little wonder there has been such a huge decline in the past twenty-five years.

However, financial advisers don't do themselves any favours either!

Although this book is primarily aimed at financial advisers, the principle of leaving an employed position to pursue self-employment applies to all business owners. The life principles you need to take are the same.

A lifestyle adviser business is a business that is set up primarily by a sole trader financial adviser with the aim of sustaining a particular level of income and no more; or to provide a foundation from which to enjoy a particular lifestyle.

What exactly are you?

An obscurity of the two polar adviser business models has developed over the last five years that needs to be clearly defined. The majority of new or small firms fall somewhere between a lifestyle adviser business and a multi-adviser directly authorised business model, and finding where you fit on this spectrum is essential to achieving your future goals. Before you decide whether you're a lifestyle adviser or a directly authorised multi-adviser startup entrepreneur, you have to understand the difference between the two and why it matters.

Starting a business is ultimately about personal fulfillment. Financial advisers who start a self-employed financial adviser business do so because they want to make their lives more appealing.

This could mean a more flexible working week, a less stressful working environment, the potential to earn more money, or achieving life goals. But what are you trying to achieve exactly?

To understand, let's firstly consider a directly authorised start-up business model. Start-ups are built by entrepreneurs who have a desire to find meaning in their lives and make contributions to the financial services industry. They arise out of an entrepreneur's desire to improve an existing model, system or process. Though there may be lifestyle benefits that come from building a start-up, these entrepreneurs are primarily interested in making an impact. For example, Truly Independent Ltd was set up as a multi-adviser business to support self-employed financial advisers on a contract for services basis and to clearly redefine the meaning of being a truly independent financial adviser in line with the retail distribution review. My co-director and I no longer provide financial advice. Instead, we support our advisers in what they do. Our aim was to establish Truly Independent Ltd not just to claim we are truly independent, but to define it.

A start-up business has a disruptive objective – you can't change the world by following a crowd. Startups require succeeding in an entirely different way from everyone else in the market. The risks are higher, as are the chances of failure. Such an entrepreneurial start-up adviser firm must, by definition, be directly authorised, in that it is not there to rely on others but to define its own place in financial services. Networks (and the AR model) do not support a start-up business properly but instead only mask a lifestyle business as a start-up. The AR model floats aimlessly between the two poles of a lifestyle adviser and a DA firm.

In contrast, with a sole trader lifestyle adviser business (RI), success and comfort are more important than having an effect on an industry, and the risks are lower. With no staff, no management and only regulation to abide by, being a lifestyle adviser is a safer bet by following the crowd and then outperforming them. The purpose is simply to enjoy what you're doing.

A lifestyle adviser business is best positioned through a well-established 'umbrella' style adviser support firm, such as Truly Independent Ltd. There are no start-up costs as compared to Direct Regulation – you simply join the established firm as a registered individual.

Time to define your adviser business model

You should now be better placed to make three choices and settle on a suitable base structure on which to build your business. It could be for example:

1 Directly authorised | Restricted advice | Sole trader lifestyle model
2 Registered individual | Independent advice | Sole trader lifestyle model
3 Directly authorised | Independent advice | Multi-adviser model

Whichever type of business model you decide on, it's also important to clearly define why you're interested in starting (or running) a self-employed business in the first place. Knowing why you're in business will also give you the confidence and motivation you need to make it a happy journey and therefore successful.

To maintain a sense of clarity, ask yourself the following seven questions to see whether you're closer to being a lifestyle adviser or a directly authorised start-up multi-adviser financial adviser firm:

1 Which is more important to you: a better lifestyle or a sense of purpose?
2 How significant is your preference for more freedom and time or ambition and prominence?
3 Are you willing to lose everything or risk little?
4 What will you do to fund your business and satisfy Capital Adequacy or do you prefer minimal cost?
5 Can you work alone or prefer to be part of something already established?
6 Are you willing to make sacrifices for the next three to five years to accomplish your goals, or do you demand immediate success?

7 What does success look like to you; do you want to be shown or do you want to show others?

Answering these questions and establishing purpose removes any illusions (or delusions) about being a self-employed financial adviser.

Carefully consider your answers to these issues, as neither option is easy. There's no shortcut to creating your own business, and there are different paths you can take, depending on your motivations.

The sad truth is that many multi-adviser firms rarely go beyond about five advisers in total. This low number achieves very little for the founding principal, not even decent profits for the enormous effort. Usually, the principal of the firm will find that time to review his own clients diminishes and instead, he ends up a manager.

We have already had six such small DA firms that have closed their doors and joined us as individual RIs, and today they are making more net income than they did as principals, without the stress. To break even against the increased time and costs for a growing multi-adviser firm, you need more like twelve advisers. Further, you need greater than twenty advisers to start making a reasonable profit. It's tough to make a dent in this industry, so the choice is stark. You either settle for the sole trader lifestyle business, or you cease advising and aim to grow a national IFA.

Setting your structure at the outset is vital since as many have experienced, there is no prize for betwixt and between.

Our approach to structure

We looked at all available models back in 2009 and settled on the idea of:

- direct authorisation and supported by our own internal compliance department;
- multi-adviser firm expanding to 100 self-employed registered individuals, nationally; and
- all offering truly independent financial advice, on a sole trader lifestyle model.

We are committed to maintaining the ethos of providing friendly *truly* independent financial advice without being adversely governed or influenced by others.

We support sole trader lifestyle choice independent financial adviser (IFA) businesses that are self-managed by the registered individuals with the aim of sustaining a certain level of income or to provide a basis from which to enjoy a happy lifestyle.

Since RDR, most firms have abandoned the independent advice model for the apparent leaner restricted model. Over time we know they will lose clients to either:

- independents such as us, or
- direct self-investment models (including robo-advice)

We have strength, no debts and are very profitable. We know financial advisers will return to more lucrative IFA models that offer more specialist and more lucrative impartial advice. In fact, the greatest reason advisers are moving to us, is one of restricted versus independent models. In contrast, Truly Independent was set up in 2010 with these regulatory changes in mind and hence has no legacy, compliance or economic issues to improve.

We are directly responsible for the advice given by our financial advisers, and that makes us more cautious, which is the right protection for them and is in our best interests. Our compliance department makes all regulatory decisions by gathering information from all available sources and acting on that. We read everything and then make decisions based on our findings and our own interpretation of the facts.

We are well established, have a strong foundation and strong structure in place to grow and develop.

Step 2. Strategy
Start With The End In Mind

'*Without strategy, execution is aimless. Without execution, strategy is useless.*'
Morris Chang
CEO of TSMC

Businesses exist because someone, maybe you, needs to make money. It is the number one driver of any business.

When a business stops making money, the doors close. And most businesses close because the business lacked a realistic strategy. No real understanding as to why they exist and worse, if they can survive long term or how they will exit into retirement.

Yet despite this, many business owners still fail to plan. Even the best financial advisers fail to plan their self-employed business adventure. I have witnessed their failures and seen their very financial demise due to a combination of bad planning and mismanagement, but mostly because they had no direction. A journey without an end goal is a journey without ambition. All too often I witness this aimless journey for many new financial advice business owners. They tend to live in the short term ideology without consideration for the journey or the end. Their only consideration is:

1 To have their own business name, logo and stationery
2 To go into business with their family or financial adviser friends
3 To make more money because they think they will
4 To be their own boss because they think life will be better
5 To do something else because they decide any change is progress

This is a front-end strategy with no consideration of how to grow, how to profit or how to exit. This is not the strategy you need to adopt. It serves no purpose to everyday activities, business measures, funding, growth plans, staffing costs, compliance functions, case checking and supervision, daily business costs, etc. Put simply, not having a proper long term business strategy is blind hope.

What is needed is a strategy that achieves an end goal. Start with the end in mind and make sure you are building a business with an exit plan. No matter if your structure is an individual lifestyle business or a larger multi-adviser business, the strategy to adopt must come from these three considerations:

1   Where are you now? (What do you start with, your strengths and weaknesses)
2   Where do you want to be? (In two years, five years, ten years and how to exit)
3   How do you get there? (What needs to change to overcome barriers, improve and develop)

You need a strategy that achieves an end goal

An appropriate strategy defines your vision and goals. Strategy is the foundation on which your development will grow. Nothing will become clear until you have a strategy to execute. A sound and purposeful strategy is one that sets out the eventual outcome and lays down clear rules and learning stages on the journey to your target. A strategy without a target is just a random walk. So a starting strategy has to consider both the journey and the final outcome, or outcomes. But it also has to be flexible and accommodating over time, unlike the basic structure which must remain steadfast.

A good strategy fully executed is better than a great strategy partially executed. A good strategy needs to be followed through to achieve the desired outcome. It follows that your full execution of the strategy is key to your success, but you must also be able to monitor your progress.

Every strategy requires a set of rules to follow, a process to follow and procedures to abide by. Working without process and procedure is irresponsible strategy departure and causes deviation and irregularity. Just as it is damaging not to adhere to regulatory process and procedures, it is equally damaging not to have and adhere to your own business growth process and procedure strategy.

Every day should be your best day

To explain this strategy, allow an analogy. We have all bought cars, houses, and furniture. Also, we have probably all sold those cars, houses, and furniture. When we buy these items as new, we care for them, protect them, we admire them.

Later on, when we come to sell them again, we ensure the buyer sees these items in the best possible condition, subject to acceptable aging. We de-clutter, clean and polish those things to make them more attractive to a buyer and to hopefully obtain the best possible price. This is normal and expected.

However, during the middle years of ownership of these items, we tend to lose interest following those early days of care and protection. We allow the car to go unwashed and fill with empty sweet wrappers. We allow the house to be used as a dumping ground for bikes, shoes, newspapers and other such stuff. We allow our prize possessions to be damaged and unfixed.

You cannot treat your business this way. Every day in business should be your best day. Build your business as if you were presenting it for sale, that year, that month, that week, that day. Your business plan (hence your strategy) should be written down and improved as you improve. It is essential to keep your business tidy, clean, lean and attractive to a buyer. Be the best, show the rest.

It is essential therefore, that part of your strategy is to have a running prospectus for your business. It does not need to be lengthy, but informative with a bullet point structure. To list just a few areas to include:

- A short bio about you and your achievements
- Your business structure and strategy
- Outline the systems you have in place
- Include your client service proposition
- Where you are supported, and by whom
- Provide an overview of your last three years' accounts, turnover, gross and net profit

- The total number of your clients and the areas they reside
- The total number of new clients each year and their source
- The amount of new business each year against ongoing business
- The total number of assets under advice (AuA)
- The average number of AuA per client
- The time you spend on your business, both marketing, and existing client business

In doing this, you are providing a service to your business. This prospectus may never see the eye of another for many years, but you know your strengths and weaknesses. Further, you will be able to place a value on your business, ready for sale, every day. In doing this exercise, you have started with the end in mind.

The broader strategy

Any business has two primary and related economic business measures. They are 'Business Efficiency' and 'Marketing Effectiveness'. One does not exist without the other and is all too often ignored by small firms as business jargon, though well written about in business studies and used by CEOs of large businesses and defined in Dictionary.com as:

Effective (adj.) – Adequate to accomplish a purpose; producing the intended or expected result.

Efficient (adj.) – Performing or functioning in the best possible manner with the least waste of time and effort.

Efficiency is doing things right, effectiveness is doing the right things.
Peter F. Drucker

Quite often the business focus is on turnover, gross profit, and net profit as being the best business measures. If you wanted to buy a business or invest in a business then, of course, the business accounts matter a great deal, but they don't always help the business owner to grow their business. A set of business accounts can tell you if you made a profit or not, or how much you spend to run your business or how much tax you have to pay, but they don't provide a solution to those running issues. If there is no profit, what do you do? If it costs too much to run the business what do you do? If your finances are stretched, then what do you do?

There are two simple measures that every business can use to determine their progress, which is current and not reliant on a set of accounts to provide the information.

Measure your business progress

The *Happy Financial Adviser* uses two nifty calculations to measure their business efficiency and their marketing effectiveness. These are used to determine progress and to identify weaknesses:

1 Business efficiency – Calculate your client efficiency rate
2 Marketing effectiveness – Calculate your new client ratio

These two business measures are strongly related. We all have a weekly time constraint, so one of these business measures does not change without the other being affected. They are economically linked. The more effective you are in marketing and promoting your business, the more efficient you need to be, to deliver on that promise.

As a financial adviser, if you focus on marketing activity and generate plenty of new business, or indeed provide an ongoing service proposition that generates high-income streams, then you need to be very efficient in how you process that business. In these circumstances, without an efficient business model in place, you will be heading for a client crunch – a limit point where you have no time to advise new clients. Such time-consuming limits are common these days, post-RDR, as self styled 'wealth management' firms lead the way in the provision of elaborate ongoing servicing strategies for their clients.

The most common response to such time constraints is to employ more staff. However, Staff need training, to be mentored, monitored and paid, which all leads to more stress on profits, existing staff and the business as a whole. Most firms like this end up being sold to consolidators in a vain attempt to reduce risk to the owners and alleviate stress from time constrained business. Employment of more staff is not always the solution.

Let us explore each of business efficiency and marketing effectiveness in turn, and their respective ways to calculate and measure progress.

BUSINESS EFFICIENCY

To achieve business efficiency does not mean you have to go down the 'restricted advice' model, it is more about the technology, processes, and procedures that are adopted and less about your advice range. Our focus on process has meant we are extremely efficient for a firm which adopts the unbiased and unrestricted truly independent model.

Efficiency through technology

The way to maintain your business efficiencies is by use of the best available technology to do the work for you. The best technology costs more. When considering technology for your business, don't be fooled into low cost. Think primarily about function and business efficiency. Consider the time you will save by adopting an excellent back office system, the control you will have and the added value to your business.

Being efficient, not only in the function of advising your clients but as a firm on back office issues, will allow you to adapt quickly to necessary change. If you are a multi-adviser firm, such efficiency means you could pay your financial advisers more as you need less money to run the firm. This, in turn, can be passed on to clients, where required.

Desire to be efficient

An efficient business can charge fees for business advice on a percentage basis, not time for money. Some financial adviser firms charge clients by the hour for their advice but actually, charging an hourly rate is restrictive to growth. They claim to be fairer to clients because they charge an hourly rate but this is a misguided belief because the more efficient they become, the less they charge their clients. Therefore, there is no desire to be efficient which means these firms simply take longer to conclude a piece of advice business.

The argument is that a firm that charges 3% of an investment of say £50,000 (£1,500) is overcharging and that charging an hourly rate is better. However, an hourly rate of £150 yields the same fee if they charge the client ten hours of time. At Truly Independent Ltd, the more efficient our advisers become, the greater their hourly rate. By engaging with the right technology, there is a reward for efficiency. In contrast, a firm who charges an hourly rate has no incentive to be efficient. In this example, if they increased efficiency and were able to reduce the ten hours down to six hours (£900), it would cost the firm £600. The reason why most who charge by the hour remain inefficient.

Calculate your client efficiency rate

A sole trader financial adviser working from home can measure how efficient he is by recording the actual hours he spends on specific client business. Each month, record the time you leave the house for a client meeting, the time you spend in the meeting and the return journey. Record the time you take to process the data collected, the research and collation of any documentation. Include the return meeting to present your recommendations and the full implementation of the business right up to the point of completion and payment. This is your client time and should be recorded for both new and existing business. Make sure you ignore the time you spend on general business tasks such as replacing the printer ink or ordering new business cards or time spent on continual professional development or listening to webinars, none of which are client time-specific.

In the same month divide your total gross income generated from client fees by your client time to determine your business efficiency measure – your client efficiency rate.

This is nothing to do with the 'hourly rate' you may charge your clients and everything to do with your efficiency. At a recent event, we asked a small group of financial advisers to calculate their 'client efficiency rate' based upon a single £15,000 client investment. Their client efficiency rates varied from £45 per hour to £100 per hour. There were only two factors, how much they charge and the time spent on the task.

Interestingly, the adviser on £100 per hour client efficiency rate charged the client 4% (£600) of the investment and took six hours to complete the task. In contrast, the adviser on £45 per hour charged the client 3% (£450) and took ten hours to complete the task.

In the interest of fairness, one adviser had a client efficiency rate of £60 per hour having charged 4% (£600) but took ten hours to complete the task. While he is comfortable with charging a higher amount for his advice, he lacks the business efficiency skills and could learn from others.

There is no right or wrong answer here, but it does highlight that business efficiency is not about what you charge or how you charge, but more importantly it's the time you take to complete the task. Advisers can monitor their own development this way and seek to make improvements in their efficiency.

You can keep your charges down to a more competitive rate if the time spent is minimal. Even a 2% charge of

£300, in this example, would yield a client efficiency rate of £60 per hour if the client time was minimised to five hours. Equally, four hours would yield £75 per hour. Not bad for a small case.

It follows then that if you can become very efficient regarding client time, then you can either charge less to market yourself better or maintain your percentage charging rates, making you more money per hour.

In the last example, we were able to reduce the charges for a small, simple investment case by simply improving the business efficiency, termed the client efficiency rate. This allows the financial adviser to be more competitive when need be and more open to giving much needed Financial Advice to the less well off. Why restrict your market?

We encourage every financial adviser to divide their monthly fee income by the hours they spend on client specific time that month to obtain their client efficiency rate. The idea being that by comparing, you can measure to improve.

In fact, to name a few benefits, being more efficient means you:

- can adopt an independent model, the client's choice;
- are able to adapt quickly to necessary change;
- charge fees for business, not time for money;
- have a business model that is attractive to buyers;

- put client-specific research ahead of due diligence;
- never have to work for product providers as their lackey;
- give time to be in business to improve lives and not just for personal gain; and
- spend time with clients to understand their true financial needs better.

MARKETING EFFECTIVENESS

Now that you have mastered the need of business efficiency to reduce your time spent on business, effectively increasing your hourly rate in the process, what will you do with that added time?

With this newly added time freedom, you could take the time to play golf or take other exercise. Maybe spend time with your friends and family. You could take a holiday.

Or, you could use this added time to connect with more clients and market yourself more effectively. In essence, time saved with some clients will make time for others.

New clients, new business

If you have mastered an efficient business process for all product areas, you are ready to take on any new business that comes your way. You have increased new business capacity. The more efficient you are, the more effective you can be with your marketing strategy.

You have simply found yourself some time. Having time is essential to market yourself, to make people aware of who you are and what you can do to help them. It can be fun.

The best recommendations to new client contacts come from good connections with existing clients, introducers and other people you meet as your community activities increase. You will also acquire new clients if you remain alert.

Client referrals

The best way to market your business is direct to existing clients and to always ask for referrals. This may be old information, but very few financial advisers today ask for referrals, because they no longer have a manager prompting them to do so. It's the best way for growth, it's the cheapest marketing method, and a referral from existing clients is an incredibly warm referral. You can structure a referral request into a simple service standards questionnaire (e.g. Would you recommend our IFA service to others?).

Introducer referrals

Introductions to your service from other professionals such as solicitors or accountants are another great way to connect with high net worth individuals needing advice. Such professionals will tend only to introduce to independent financial advisers, in a way to ensure they remain unbiased in their introduction.

Too many financial advisers give up on securing such lucrative relationships from introducing professionals after just a few attempts to entice them. It is important to make your service available at regular intervals until they bite. Try an email campaign, or even better, send out newsletters and printed magazines to demonstrate that you're professional too – persistence always pays off. Drop in one of your company branded magazines to their reception today and every month until someone connects with you.

Branding

Use a brand name with a meaning that clients can relate to or understand. Some financial advisers use brand names that are nothing short of a 'riddle.' Giving your business a name that requires explanation is not clever, it's a marketing opportunity lost. You are not Google!

Calculate your new client ratio

Just like the 'client efficiency rate' which is a measure of your ability to process new and existing business with ease, your marketing effectiveness can be equally measured.

This time, the amount of income is not relevant since it is new clients that you want and their business levels vary. Hence the right measure is the consideration of the number of new clients as a ratio of existing clients. Quite often, it is existing client recommendations that produce new clients, so a ratio of the two allows you to visualise both in the same figure.

For example, if you have 120 existing clients and you take on 12 more in the next 12 months, you have 12:120 or expressed at the lowest common denominator, your new client ratio would be 1:10 (for every one new client you have 10 existing clients). You now have 120 + 12 = 132 clients.

The following year say, you might expand further by another 12 new clients, so your new client ratio will be 12:132 or expressed as 1:11.

In this example, you have taken on the same number of clients increasing to 144 but your marketing effectiveness has decreased from 1:10 to 1:11. You could argue that your 12 new clients last year did not introduce you to their family of friends, or their own social networks which might be your fault in failing to ask.

Without such a ratio to measure your effectiveness, you would not be able to address the issues that impact on your business growth. A client's social network today is bigger than ever before and not asking for their endorsement or recommendation is a hugely missed opportunity; an opportunity cost.

In the example above, to get back close to a 1:10 ratio, you would need 14 new clients to provide the ratio of 14:144. Hopefully, you have recognised that a constant ratio is a growing ratio and 1:10 is a fair target measure for any growing small or sole trader business.

There are no rules to effective marketing. There is no right or wrong way to be effective in the marketing of your services, other than ensuring that whatever you do, it works for you. But make sure you regularly analyse the ratio of new clients to existing clients so see if your marketing methods are working.

To ensure you are effective in marketing, you should

- have an effective social and business pitch;
- always carry your business cards and marketing material to take advantage of every opportunity;
- promote a brand name with meaning that clients can relate to and understand;
- develop impressive communication skills, in business and socially;
- always ask for referrals;

- publish blogs on websites on a regular basis and get involved;
- use social media as a marketing tool to promote your services, not just your own web page;
- never waste money on ineffective advertising; and
- never wait for introductions – seek introducers first.

Our approach to strategy

Truly Independent is a national IFA and our long-term strategy is to grow through the recruitment of high-quality and dedicated financial advisers into our ready-made business. We are a lifestyle adviser support business.

Our end strategy is to grow in such a way that the co-founders can exit out the top without the sale of the company. With such a strategy, my co-founder and I will benefit from strong dividends, and the financial advisers who join us will benefit from the security of knowing that our successors are promoted from within. We have already made good progress to encourage staff promotion into responsible management positions and further into director positions to ensure longevity. This way, financial advisers who join us will be sure of this firm remaining *truly* in control.

Personally, I have already made the significant transition from working in the business to working on the business. This has allowed me to focus on marketing development to support further recruitment. The next stage of our development is to focus on marketing for new clients for our IFAs. Our strong drive towards business efficiency has released time constraints, and our advisers are now well placed to welcome new clients.

When it comes to effective marketing, the best brand names are those that tell the client exactly what you do. That is why we chose 'Truly Independent financial advice for everyone' as our brand name and strapline. All our advisers use this brand to market their services, and we are poised to increase our exposure to social media in a big way.

Step 3. Systems

Match Your Business To The Right Technology

*'Everything must be made as simple as possible.
But not simpler.'*
Albert Einstein

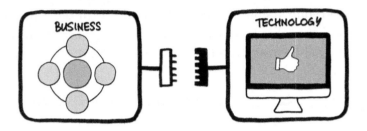

Having defined your business core structure and set out your strategy, you are now ready to put some IT systems in place to match them.

You have completed the Transition Zone and are now entering the Happy Zone. The next trio of steps, being systems, services, and support are all aligned with the three happy determinants:

- Systems: connection with more people
- Services: making a difference
- Support: having the freedom to be yourself

Simple systems

The systems you select for your business should be simple to use but always pushing the boundary of IT evolution. They have to satisfy every eventuality, especially if you are an IFA. There is nothing wrong with complex providing the system is not complicated and has simple processes within. Think of it as being like the road network in the UK, which is complex and virtually impossible to visualise all at once, but thankfully you don't need to. Generally, you only need to worry about the road you are on, which is unlikely to be complicated; taken one mile at a time. In financial advice terms, the most efficient recommendation can be accompanied by the use of the part of the system that provides the least resistance.

Let's say you want to maintain a client efficiency rate of £100 per hour, then you will need a system complex enough to satisfy these two extremes, for example:

1   A recommendation to invest a single £10,000 into an ISA, with the client assessed as balanced risk and being charged a 4% (£400) fee, which means that four hours would be your maximum process time, and which will require a slick throughput of the process to implementation.
2   In contrast, a recommendation to consolidate five smaller pensions into a single flexible pension facility, with over £500,000 of pension fund assets, charging 0.5% (£2500) will require a more complex process to implementation, giving you a maximum process time of twenty-five hours.

As you learned in the chapter on strategy, there is no point in planning to build a multi-adviser firm without considering the end target. It is important to imagine what the firm will look like in the future and when. That way, you can select the right software for your business.

Equally, if you are planning on being a sole trader, independent financial adviser who works primarily from home, then the technology has to suit your chosen business model. There is overlap, of course, since a multi-adviser business will need technology software suitable to satisfy the needs of their sole trader financial advisers.

Systems can be extremely complicated or incredibly simple, but the best systems cost money and as stated before, you should avoid cheap, as many systems do not cover every eventuality.

Matching technology to your business model

How do you make a financial adviser business a commercial success?

A successful business model is about robust growth and profit. Advice firms that have the ambition to grow 'significantly' will need to grow 'efficiently' and in all three areas of, adviser numbers, client numbers, and staff numbers. For significant success, an efficient correlation between these three areas must exist, and significant growth in one area cannot survive without growth in the other.

If you are a sole trader business, then you probably are so because of the lifestyle you can have. When working, you will want to be focused on your clients and not on non-client-specific matters. It follows, therefore that the system you require should allow you to process both complex client cases as well as brisk simple business for the smaller, straightforward cases.

In contrast, a multi-adviser business will need all of the above for their advisers, but also a back office system that efficiently manages the non-client aspects of the business.

Client-centred business

Most firms typically start out as a two-person adviser business and grow by increasing client numbers which eventually leads to a need for more administrative staff. They continue to grow their client numbers and resulting administrative staff numbers until a point where they need to recruit advisers to handle the increased client numbers. These advisers are usually employed. This hypothetical firm is a good business and is 'client-centred.' It is the most common and tends to grow by reacting to demands rather than by design.

Client-centred businesses tend not to support self-employed advisers since the focus is on the clients and not the advisers. Client-centered models tend to have high staff numbers and in many cases more than adviser numbers. This model can have expansion constraints, and few have grown significantly large. They are typically limited to being local and tend to work from a single office, with an occasional branch office some miles away. The ratio of advisers to staff could be as close as 10:10 or even skewed towards staff.

In this business, the financial advisers see their clients and the firm's staff take care of all the other client associated administration, known in the industry as para-planning.

The software for this type of business is, therefore, more focused on paraplanning support rather than financial adviser support. It is likely that ongoing client relations are conducted by staff rather than the financial adviser.

Adviser-centred business

In contrast, a multi-adviser model grows by the recruitment and support of financial advisers. It is a proactive model which gives more time and money to the financial advisers by use of advanced IT systems. Growth is well planned by design, not reaction to demand.

Clients are supported indirectly through their advisers by use of efficient business systems while the firm supports the advisers directly. Adviser centered growth is the right model for self-employed advisers and has no restriction on territory since online systems mean advisers don't need to be local, allowing for countrywide expansion.

Having established two unique business models, what are key areas of general importance to make a self-employed multi-adviser firm a success?

To achieve commercial success, the directors must:

1 Develop an 'adviser centred' business plan, and not advise
2 Plan for and adopt the right IT systems for the purpose
3 Provide an attractive proposition to advisers to aid recruitment

Technology has to be at the heart of both business models, but with differing needs. Adviser centered businesses tend to expand to greater adviser numbers, typically on a self-employed contract for services, are national in distribution and will have a greater reliance on a remote system. In contrast, the client-centered model will typically need software that is localised to the office and more geared to paraplanning support.

Both systems have minimum cross-over needs, but there are differences, if not considered from day one, could limit growth without suitable change later on. Getting the right business model and then the right software to fit that model is vital. It is crucial to choose the right growth plan, either client-centered or adviser centered, but never, never, never both.

The wrong model or bad software is a barrier to business and can cause problems down the line. To solve this potential bottleneck, take the time to plan your intended lifestyle and ask yourself these questions:

- Do I want a multi-adviser business?
- Do I want to continue to advise my client's long term?
- Do I want national expansion and remote advisers?
- Do I want to employ advisers or run a self-employed proposition?
- Do I want an easier and happier life, as a financial adviser, working from home without the hassle?

To run a successful adviser centered business you will have to implement the use of no fewer than six technological advanced systems to help you coordinate a complete IT package, all individually useful but collectively very powerful.

Back-office systems

Multi-adviser firms need an IT system that is powerful and comprehensive. Such a back office system should run everything efficiently and when appropriate, automatically. All data entered should be on a single data entry basis to increase efficiency, without the need to repeat entries all the way through to case completion.

The system should be completely paperless. All client specific information, personal documents, and policy details need to be stored on a single system together with your client fact find data, any conducted research, and other related files. There should be no storage limits and no limits to the number of users on such a system.

Put simply, everything you need to do business should be just a click away. Use of integrated planning tools will make life easier and hep you to quickly produce suitability reports without the need for para-planning support.

Access to your system should be from anywhere, whenever and wherever you are. Any financial adviser, anywhere in the country, should be able to get access to the system online, from home or office base with a simple login. Some systems are only suitable for local office environments and have been slow to update to modern demands. A system that is 100% online will allow financial advisers to access it country wide, and so allow ease of expansion.

Mobile technology

Everything today is on the go. To ensure you provide a modern financial advice experience, ahead of robo-advice, it is becoming essential to utilise mobile applications. Such systems will allow you, to manage client data, from anywhere. An office is not required. You should ensure you can operate your business from anywhere in the world from a PC, laptop, tablet or mobile device.

Website

There should be the main website aimed at the new client. It should be modern and mobile friendly, easy to find and with enough traffic to respond to searches. A potential new client should be able to find a financial adviser in their local area.

Possible new clients should be able to access financial calculators, fact sheets, magazines, and guides from this website, if only to entice and to demonstrate the firm's credibility and authority. Fresh news articles relating to current political and financial matters should be published. Your website should be the window to your firm and full of assets for new clients and existing clients.

Clients should also use this website to access a client web portal.

Client web portal

This is a private client login to their own personal web pages where they can access real time valuations of their investments and pensions. If you are independent, then their valuations from a variety of product providers and firms should also be available through this single client web portal.

As already stated, most clients only need to know two things about their savings and investments:

1 What is the valuation today?
2 Is the investment still right for me?

A good system should be able to answer those two questions without the Client's financial adviser needing to be consulted. This would be both extremely useful for the client and efficient time saving for the financial adviser.

Systems exist where clients can log in and obtain an almost immediate valuation of their investment and pension plans and at the same time provide projections to their plan targets and goals.

Social media connection

You will appreciate the value of referrals from existing clients as a solid and low-cost method of marketing your financial advice services. Next, to that, is ensuring you have a connection with social media platforms. They are the fastest growing areas for marketing your business and while many firms use this technology to promote their products and services, the financial advisers I meet have not yet embraced this phenomenon.

An alternative to asking for your existing clients to make a direct referral to you of a family member or friend is to ask them instead to promote you on their social media page, such as Facebook. It is a sure way to build multiple connections and hence multiple referrals.

All your existing client has to do is to state something like, 'I received some precious pensions advice this week, from my financial adviser www.trulyonline.co.uk.' Of course, you then need an effective landing page to capture those referrals that will follow.

Email and communication

Good communication with your clients is vital to your success. In this highly interactive world, your clients will expect their financial advisers to engage in quick replies to problems, to return telephone calls, emails and text. There is a substantial difference between the workings of a business email facility and a personal email facility. Do not set up a business with a private email service and instead make sure it is specific for business use. It also follows, that secure systems of communication are even better.

Multi-adviser intranet

Connecting with fellow financial advisers though a firm's own private intranet provides much-needed support from each other. Group and individual conversations, answers to technical questions, firm announcements and social interaction all help to cement a firms brand.

A firm's own intranet will allow financial advisers to share ideas, stories, and problems. A problem shared is a problem halved. With such technology systems in place, financial advisers will always be connected to the firm, to each other, information and conversations.

Added-value resources and external software

Good IT systems don't just stop at the back office system, the email system, website, and intranet. There are plenty of alternative IT systems that some financial advisers need, which will provide much added value to their business. Such alternative systems are plentiful and while many are not all are necessary, some are very useful tools, such as:

- a plethora of platforms.
- research fund websites
- comparison systems for personal and define benefit pensions
- life insurance and mortgage comparison quoting systems
- product comparison systems
- cash flow software systems
- 'Find an Adviser' search systems

It is important to note, never rely on software for research solutions alone. There has been too much reliance on software to make client decisions which remove the soft facts which may be more significant to a client recommendation that just software comparisons.

Our approach to systems

We are an adviser-centred firm. We adopted our IT systems primarily for our financial advisers, but all consideration made with their clients in mind. Our business strategy is to focus on being efficient with the use of the best available IT systems on the market today.

The correct use of technology means we can minimise adviser costs. Our whole model (and a measure of efficiency) is based upon an adviser to staff ratio of 10:1. For 100 advisers, we only need ten staff, and that is down primarily to technological efficiency and good design.

Efficient client top-ups via ImpulseSave®

To be efficient is to provide a system for both our financial advisers and their clients. The most impressive of which is a unique client saving facility applying only to existing plans where advice has previously been given. It does not remove the adviser relationship and should not be confused with direct investment. It is a recommendation and advice facility.

For any advice business to exist today, there are large minimum fixed charges from regulators, PI insurers and technology protection and support. This is one reason why we have to charge a minimum advice fee (currently £360) for every single advice case, and many other firms do similar. Our basic rule is, if there is a recommendation, there is a minimum fee.

Currently, this means, low monetary additions to year end ISAs would incur a minimum £360 advice fee. For example, £3,600 additional investment would incur a minimum fee of £360 which is effectively an advice fee of 10%. This is exactly the barrier to savings for the less well-off and who need advice. However, our client web portal provides a brilliant solution to this problem. It is called ImpulseSave® and available through our back-office software which is award winning and provided to us by True Potential LLP.

When recommending savings and investment plans, every financial adviser worth their salt, should anticipate future additional investments at the outset. Indeed, this is what your main advice focus should be about. As I have already touched on and will explain more thoroughly in the next chapter about services, being an adviser today is more about explaining asset accumulation and less asset allocation. By doing this, you can provide a long-term saving relationship with your client to accumulate assets in an extremely efficient manner; and build that potential into your suitability letters (i.e. recommend the invest-ment now and future *ad hoc* investment, all covered in the same client suitability letter).

As an example:

'I recommend you invest an affordable £12,000 into your ISA this year. To maximise your ISA allowance, you can add a further £3,240 before the year end (2016/17) which you are expecting to fund from work-related bonuses. I therefore further recommend you invest in an ISA on our integrated Investment Platform which includes an online client facility to add to your investment when your bonus is paid. Should you use this facility in the future, there will be an initial fee of 1% applied to any additional investment.'

In all consideration, financial advisers need to embrace the use of such advanced technology to enhance their business. This client top-up facility is a fantastic tool to help all financial advisers to get one step ahead of robo-Advice and to maintain that client adviser relationship. Make your recommendation to include a client 'top-up' facility before others and still get paid for providing that facility.

In the £3,600 example above, the client could use our top-up facility to increase their investment online through the web portal and incur just £36 initial charge rather than the £360 minimum our financial advisers would have to charge for advice. This is both a cost saving for your client and time efficient for you – time needed to focus on obtaining new clients where the real value is.

Step 4. Services

More Asset Accumulation,

Less Asset Allocation

> 'The main reason people struggle financially is
> because they have spent years in school but
> learned nothing about money. The result is that
> people learn to work for money ...but never
> learn to have money work for them.'
>
> **Robert Kiyosaki**
> Author

Financial advisers in the UK today need to change and
improve the way they work.

Just ten years ago, a financial adviser would express their importance and value regarding product knowledge, including the tax rules, the investment limits, maximums and minimums, what you can and cannot do. This is no longer of any value to anyone because of Google.

Put simply, we can Google anything. ISA limits, pension limits, inheritance tax and trust information – it's all there and available in seconds. We are all plugged into a world wide web of information, which is astonishing to behold!

In 2013, many financial advisers moved away from traditional advice models and developed a 'wealth management' approach instead. They have abandoned the independent model in favour of the seemingly less complex restricted model to alleviate the rising cost of regulation. It's a classic error to give up and ignore some of your tools (financial products) in an attempt to reduce business expense associated with being independent.

Equally, the end of commission and the introduction of charging fees for client advice worried many advisers. This led to the invention of a host of unnecessary and highfalutin ongoing service propositions which include, for example, six-monthly rebalancing, six-monthly adviser reviews, account managers services, discretionary fund services, newsletters and personalised market reports. All to make up the commission difference in the guise of a needed ongoing service and postulated the so-called Wealth Management model.

But the truth is that clients are paying more for ongoing advice today, by the back door, than they ever did on commission trail. I am aware of clients paying from 1% up to 1.75% for ongoing service charges to adviser firms, when ongoing commission was typically 0.5%, excluding fund manager and platform fees. It's impressive sales to persuade clients to take up a service that is expensive and in most cases not needed!

The savings crunch

When advisers stopped focussing on savings shortfalls with clients, the savings gap started. All too often financial advisers think their job is to turn a given sum of money into a bigger sum of money and they end up spending far too much effort on fund selection, fund performance, portfolio construction and portfolio management. That is the job of the fund manager, not the financial adviser.

Financial advisers need to change their tactics. They need to stop talking about products and start explaining shortfall. There is a savings gap which is the next economic time bomb – let's call it the savings crunch. Despite the credit crunch back in 2008, access to borrowing remains just as easy today. Personal debt (excluding mortgages) is growing and is now approximately 113% of average earnings. The average total debt per household (including mortgages) was £55,982 in November 2016. What is worrying, according to the Office for Budget Responsibility's November 2016 forecast, household debt is predicted to reach £2.294 trillion in Q1 2022, which makes the average household debt £84,964. (Source: The Money Charity)

Your clients deserve a new approach. Financial advisers today need to stop charging high fees for ongoing fabricated services and to instead start selling the need for their client to accumulate assets instead of liabilities.

The rich and wealthy story

The rich and wealthy generate their income from assets and not from working. Any work they do is purely for fun. They don't line the pockets of employers, they don't fund the banks through mortgages, loans, and credit card interest and they don't pay national insurances, tax or inheritance tax. Why, because their income comes from their assets. By assets, I mean property ownership, shares, investment, bonds and owning businesses.

As financial advisers, you have the position and the responsibility to ensure your clients understand the importance of saving and saving hard. Your job is to express the importance of accumulation of assets by saving their income, not spending it.

For example, an employee earning £30,000 per annum would require assets that are free to produce an income of, at least, twenty times their annual income = £600,000.

No amount of ongoing service advice and endless fund shuffling will generate that from small savings. Clients need to fund most of it, and they need to know their shortfall. If the employee had £300,000 to invest, it would still take ten years and 7.2%pa growth for the £600,000 target to be achieved and at some risk. With just £150,000 to invest, it would take twenty years at 7.2% to double twice. If you take away fund charges, platform charges and ongoing adviser charges, then the time extends even further.

Little wins

When you next explain to your client that to be wealthy enough to retire, they need say, £600,000 (20 x £30,000 per annum) plus a house to live in, they may see that as a 'no hoper' and shut down.

This message still needs to be evident as a target, just like a healthy weight is a target, a wealth of £600,000 is a target. Just as overweight people diet to lose weight, usually slowly and at a pound at a time, then those who aim for wealth need to save money, a pound at a time. Money, and little steps is the conversation to have not just wealth targets. At each saving, recognise a little win taking small steps towards wealth and health.

Every financial adviser should aim to help everyone who may be considering seeking financial advice or considering changing their current financial adviser. They should assist them to understand the industry, to know what each type of adviser can do for them, what they are permitted to do and what they quite often choose not to do. Building credibility with your clients as holding high qualifications, experience and your recognised industry status are vital to your credibility, your success and your authority. Equally, clients who know their financial adviser well and how they operate is a more powerful tool for your future security and is the creation of self-esteem. Self-esteem is an essential ingredient to making a positive difference and hence to happiness.

The secret is not to overwhelm your clients with your vast knowledge, but to chip away slowly and delicately at their economic weakness. Not having a financial adviser to call on is a weakness. Offer your card and a no obligation chat. If they agree, that is a little win.

My best clients came from little wins. The wealthy don't mind making a small investment as if to try you out. That is a little win.

The Happy Financial Adviser will encourage their clients to take control of their money and act as their guide through the financial maze. They will work with their clients to ensure they achieve their goals; each small goal achieved is a little win towards long-term financial preservation.

Today's financial adviser places too much emphasis on funds and fund selection and not enough focus on the shortfall in client capital. Clients need to stop buying debt and invest instead small or large amounts. Things don't make people happy. However, connections with others, having financial freedom and making a difference in the lives of others, does.

Encourage responsibility

To all financial advisers, instead of charging a client 1%+ for an ongoing service, reduce the charge to 0.5% and provide your client with online access to the real time value of their investment, accessible to them 24/7. Further, give them a target to achieve. Encourage them to monitor their own fund growth which will help them to save more. Your 0.5% charge should not be for ongoing adviser services which put the entire burden on you and your time, but for client web portal login access to a valuable self-monitoring system which you support, help and provide guidance. You are simply encouraging your clients to take some responsibility of their own asset accumulation.

If you do this instead, these things will happen:

- You will connect better with your client as they witness their savings grow
- They will think highly of you and be more likely to recommend a friend
- As their savings grow, so will your own income
- You will have more time to help new clients and
- You will have less stress

Consider this. It is better to have 200 clients on 0.5% ongoing charge that take up very little of your time, than 100 clients on 1% who take up most of your time... and it's a more effective business to sell on... and at a much better price.

As a financial adviser, your job is not to talk about products but instead to convince your client that to replace their employed or self-employed income, they first need to accumulate assets, after all, income follows assets.

Reluctance to change

Some advisers join our firm and soon after, we realise that they joined us to do the same thing they have always done but for a better deal. This never works and they have missed the point. It is also insane to seek improvements this way.

> 'Insanity: doing the same thing over and over again and expecting different results'.
> **Albert Einstein**

I say to them, 'If you were unhappy where you were, and you operate the same way here with us, you will be equally unhappy. There is no shortcut to happiness (or success) it takes a real commitment to change the way you think and work. But it can be achieved.'

There is an urgent need for financial advisers to drop the so-called wealth management title and return to the more productive IFA title. Your service is to encourage more saving and investment and to minimise the cost to the client in doing so.

If you have an efficient business, you have more time to connect with more people and to provide a great service, reducing the savings gap. Being independent gives you the credibility to advise on the most suitable plan for your client – it's giving you your freedom. If your client is made to understand that their challenge is to overcome their shortfall, then you will make a positive difference.

Focus on income producing assets (IPAs)

It should take no more than a few minutes of rational conversation to establish a core issue that a potential new client needs to address.

Imagine you are at a party and speaking with someone you've just been introduced to: once she has asked you what you do and identified that you are an IFA, she may ask, 'So, where is the best place to put my money?'

This is a common question but quite often not genuine. What she means, but avoided saying, could be one of the following:

- 'I have a few quid, but I'm not wealthy; should I invest?'
- 'I know about money, do you?'
- 'I am reasonably wealthy but lost confidence in my financial adviser. What are you like?'

The common thread in all these possible questions is that the person needs help.

So, your reply could be:

'It sounds like you need a little guidance or help, so allow me to explain exactly what I do. I specialise in working closely with my clients to help them to bridge their savings gap by coaching them in the accumulation of IPAs.'

'IPAs?' may be the curious reply.

'Yes. IPA means 'income producing assets'; assets to replace your income, so you don't have to work to earn it. The formula is simple: think of your income, multiply it by twenty, take away your current savings and invest-ments (or IPAs as I call them) and that gives you a figure. Yes?'

She does the mental arithmetic and says, 'Yes, I have that figure.'

'Ok,' you respond, 'that is your savings gap! So I have a question for you. What are you going to do about bridging that gap?'

I promise you, soon after you will be arranging a meeting. In just a few minutes, without paper or pen, you have identified a suitable client, they have a target in mind, a shortfall to address and you have a commitment for them to take some action. You have the start of a business relationship.

If you feel bold enough, when you are next asked what you do, answer with this:

'I specialise in coaching people to accumulate assets and bridge the savings gap.'

If you perfect this, or a similar pitch you are comfortable with, watch your client numbers grow.

In that time, you have avoided product talk, market performance and probably made that person more aware of their future challenge than their current adviser has ever done before.

By focusing on your client's shortfall (savings gap), you quickly determine a target and at the same time build a commitment to achieve it. Once a rapport is established, you are in a position to have a more formal meeting where you can assess your new client's needs in greater detail.

Ongoing servicing – an opportunity cost

Too many financial advisers today tell me they have reached capacity and cannot take on new clients. This is mainly due to the service model they have created, which tends to be cumbersome and unnecessary and one that takes too much client time, for smaller income. The level of income may be 1% ongoing, but that is still very low compared to the new business loss. Economists call this exchange an opportunity cost, since your time taken on servicing is lost to the time needed for new business. You live in a week constrained by time.

> Definition – 'Opportunity Cost,' Investopedia.com: An opportunity cost refers to a benefit that a person could have received, but gave up, to take another course of action. Stated differently, an opportunity cost represents an alternative given up when a decision is made. This cost is, therefore, most relevant to two mutually exclusive events, whereby choosing one event; a person cannot choose the other.

A financial advice business that focuses more on ongoing services to the opportunity cost of obtaining new clients and new business is losing out. Regulatory demands mean even renewal business (ongoing support) requires both formal activity and robust records just as much as any new business.

Financial advisers in our firm are waking up to the idea that building a renewal business may sound a splendid idea, but in reality, it's as much a burden on time and activity as has been the case since the mid-1990's, when regulation first insisted on a formal process.

It is, therefore, wise to make both your new business process as efficient as possible as well as the ongoing service function. As a firm, we have never adopted ongoing services and in fact have always called this proposition, ongoing support. It's a subtle difference, but just enough to emphasise to our clients that they are being supported while they take responsibility for their own financial shortfalls. An adviser's role is to focus on new business and allow technology systems to look after your ongoing client support work following your initial advice, at low cost.

Equally, you could have the most efficient business model but generate no new business. New business is the core of a strong financial adviser business and one which is being eroded by modern wealth management models as a reaction to recent regulation changes. New business generates more income than existing business and you will help more people who need your advice services and ongoing support. Don't ignore the need for new business, it's essential.

You will immediately be happier when you adopt the ethos that you are someone who is in business to make a positive difference and improve lives and not just for personal gain.

Fees and Value Added Tax (VAT)

I will be forever confused as to why financial advice firms today wish to charge clients VAT when the latest HMRC directives have provided an environment for us to work in that is VAT exempt.

When we earned our keep purely through commission, VAT was never an issue, yet now, since the switch to fees-based from commission-based advice, there has been a steady insistence of the need to charge clients VAT.

The VAT rules are simple: providing you act and advise as an Intermediary you do not need to charge VAT.

Not all, but most financial needs of the majority of clients in the UK can be solved by the supply of a suitable product in the whole of the market and therefore perfect for financial advisers to act as an intermediary when advising clients; thus providing VAT free advice.

You are able to provide your clients with VAT free advice, making your service and ongoing support service 100% VAT free. The simple rule is to act as an intermediary at all times and ensure your aim is to supply a solution to client needs.

An exempt supply of intermediary services

The official wording states:

A supplier of an exempt intermediary service is a person who:

- brings together a person seeking a financial service with a person who provides a financial service
- stands between the parties to a contract and acts in an intermediary capacity, and
- undertakes work preparatory to the completion of a contract for the provision of financial services, whether or not it is completed.

Financial service – A 'financial service' for the purposes of an 'intermediary' exemption is a service listed in the VAT Act, Schedule 9, Group 5, items 1 to 4 and 6.

Work preparatory to the completion of a contract

Work preparatory to the completion of a contract refers to work done of a specialised nature. This could include helping to set the terms of the contract or making representations on behalf of a client, but would not include work done of a general nature such as administrative or clerical formalities.

Intermediaries (independent and restricted financial advisers)

Not all financial advisers are intermediaries. Therefore, if you only provide advice and do not satisfy the 'exempt supply of intermediary' definition, then your supply is taxable.

If you give advice and act between your client and the provider of a financial product, it is important to establish which of the two elements of your service predominates. Where your advice directly results in your client taking out a financial product and you meet all the criteria for intermediary, the whole of your service – including the advice element – your charge will be exempt. The advice is seen as ancillary to an exempt intermediary service. If you receive commission from the finance product provider, it is consideration for a separate exempt supply by you of intermediary services.

If on the other hand, your advice far outweighs the work done to arrange a contract, the intermediary service is ancillary to the advice, and VAT is due on the whole supply. For example, because a client has received a general financial health-check, with advice covering a range of financial issues, but then only buys a minor product requiring minimal intermediation.

Our approach to services

We provide our financial advisers with a range of all-inclusive services for them so they can focus on their clients and this is not to be confused with the advice services our financial advisers provide for their clients.

However, for their clients, we provide a comprehensive Terms of Business that covers all the services (and support) our Advisers issue:

- Client Advice Agreement (CAA)
- Client Support Agreement (CSA)

Since 1st January 2013, I have witnessed many changes in the way we must conduct certain areas of business with our clients. Some important changes are being missed by advisers who are getting in the way of progress and all around the unshaken pre-RDR legacy mentality.

Here I want to share just twenty adviser dos and don'ts which include many of the processes we have adopted in our business and where adoption of these changes is essential to your progress too and to you providing a first class, trouble free and comprehensive client service experience.

1 Connect with clients about one thing, their lifestyle. This is the one thing a client wants to keep, their lifestyle, and the adviser needs to be interested in that lifestyle. Make a fact find discussion less about

facts and more about helping them achieve dreams and goals, likes and dislikes not just facts.

2   Find your client's lifestyle wealth figure. They have either surpassed it, so they can consider gifting or they have a shortfall, so they can consider savings and accumulating assets. Make sure you truly engage with your clients and explain the principle of enough money; that enough money is needed to fund a lifestyle and no more. Remind them that life is not a rehearsal, that time is slipping away and that all they need is enough money to sustain their chosen lifestyle or retirement. Find that figure through discussion and questioning then and only then advise on products as tools to achieve and maintain that figure.

3   Avoid the product discussion. Do not discuss products and avoid getting drawn into any product discussion. Products are tools to achieve a goal or a bigger game. Plumbers don't talk about wrenches! The game is for clients to achieve their 'enough money' figure and the goals are small steps needed to achieve the bigger game. Set goals and keep the money stuff simple.

4   Identify the right problem; there should be no products in any problem. For example, a client wanting to take tax-free cash from his pension to fund a new motor home is not a problem, it's a solution to the fact the client cannot afford to buy a motor home! The advice would be on the best way to raise funds to maintain his lifestyle. Identify the real

underlying problem and avoid product or transactional discussions.

5 Pension freedoms do not mean you are there to facilitate the client's instructions. Just because a client has read, he can take his full fund as cash doesn't mean they should. You are there to provide advice on the underlying problem, not the product. Ask, why does the client need access to his pension? Be prepared to walk away!

6 There is no such thing as a top-up. This type of discussion is a transactional product discussion which, as stated, is to be avoided. The problem is that the client wishes to invest for some reason. Identify the reason and advise. Treat all top-ups as new money. Impulsesave® is an exception to this, where previous advice has included, 'A top-up facility to help you reach your target figure (or goal) of £X in Y years'.

7 There is no such thing an 'insistent client'. Clients who insist are not clients, they should either accept the process of advice or not engage. An adviser guiding a client by way of pointing them in the right direction is deemed to have given advice. This is not financial planning!

8 If you advise on an investment vehicle, you also advise on the investment within. Advice on an investment vehicle, such as a SIPP, is also advice on the investment held. Investments must match their risk. If selling is bad, then half selling is worse!

9 There is no such thing as limited advice. All advice should be about achieving *or* maintaining a client's lifestyle, which means finding the amount of money

they need in their whole estate to have the retire-ment lifestyle they expect.

10 Fees – Initial advice and ongoing support must be mutually exclusive. One can exist without the other and future ongoing support fees should not be con-sidered as advice fees. Equally, initial advice fees must not influence the ongoing support fees.

11 Fees – All fees must be charged as per your Client Advice Agreement (CAA). A firm must decide on their client charging structure at the outset. It can be fixed, hourly or as a percentage. Truly Indepen-dent Ltd charge by percentage as other methods of charging are time constrained. Also, don't make it up at any time; charges should be as stated in the key facts or terms of business. Our minimum charge of £360 is only applied where charging the maximum 4% would produce a lower fee. Example: £8,000 in-vestment x 4% = £320, so min charge of £360 applies. All calculation must be shown on the invoice.

12 Fees – Regular contributions should first be converted. It is easier to interpret regular premium contributions (P) as a single lump sum (LS) and over how many years (T). Convert to a single lump sum and then apply your advice range. Formula 12P x T = LS, where T is maximum 10 years. Example: 12 x £150 x 10 = £18,000. Now apply your adviser charge.

13 Ongoing Support. Trail commission has gone for in-vestment and pensions. You now have to demonstrate what the client is paying for and also recording that you are providing that service. If you promise too much, you won't have time to seek new

clients and end up a servicing adviser restricted by time. Best profits come from new business, so instead focus on new business and following that with the provision of client web portals for ongoing support.

14 Auto-enrolment should only be charged for initial advice. Use the above regular premium formulae and ensure no ongoing charges to firm or individuals for ongoing support; this is controlled by the AE firms and their accounting software. Advise only on the scheme research for best fit AE solution for firms and leave them to get on with it. You can, of course, advise each member on their own lifestyle financial planning. Don't try to invent an ongoing arrangement when there is nothing to support.

15 Treating clients fairly is paramount. It is not possible to change charging for one client over another simply because you have deemed them to be 'better clients' or 'good clients'. Clients should be clients and the fees applied accordingly.

16 Demonstrate your independence. Don't restrict yourself by using the same provider/funds for every client. Choose the most appropriate products for your specific client problem whether that is driven by cost, choice, technology, service or features. Example: In the right circumstances a venture capital trust can be better than a pension to extract tax efficient funds from a business.

17 Stop trying to find an easy route. Charge the correct amount to ensure you can spend the time required to give the best advice. Explain your worth and charge for it. Clients will pay for a professional process and quality advice.

18 Risk is the key. A client can't complain about a product/fund performance but can complain about being subjected to the wrong level of risk. Make sure the product/fund matches the client's attitude to risk (ATR) and demonstrate how. The risk discussion document (RDD) is there to show your independence and is completed by the adviser at the point of making product recommendations.

19 Use all your best skills, and learn from every client meeting. Invest time in your own self-development. Improve your knowledge by reading more, learning more and bridge your own skills gap through active course attendance, not just regular CPD. This will help build confidence, build relationships and will strengthen your certainty of remaining independent. Focus not on industry skills, but personal development skill such as networking skills.

20 Market yourself though profile development, by asking your client to recommend you on their social media platform. Do you tweet, write an article, a blog, comment online, make local presentations to large or small groups, seek strong introducers to generate business, attend local network events or do you sit and wait? If you are truly independent, then use that tool/brand to open doors, and there is no better recommendation than from a happy client.

Step 5. Support
Nothing Worthwhile Is
Ever Achieved In Isolation

'Life's most persistent and urgent question is,
"What are you doing for others?" '
Martin Luther King Jr

It is important to understand that support, like service, involves two separate considerations:

1 The support *you need* to maintain an efficient business and your own development

2 The support *you give* to your clients to achieve their goals

Whatever business model you run, multi-adviser or sole trader you will need support from people who understand your business well and can take the stress away so you can focus most of you time on your clients and not on regulatory or industry generic administration. Equally, you need to ensure you have a working life that involves support from family and friends, business peers and mentors.

Your clients expect you to be their primary source of contact, to be on hand when you are needed and able to quickly respond to their needs. To achieve this, you must focus on delegating your non-client-specific business to staff and in doing so, they are supporting you. Our firm is set up specifically to support financial advisers in this role. Effectively taking away the regulatory issues and core business functions that are non-client-specific. Other Networks have a similar function but without the responsibility.

Further, at this point, it is well worth noting that administration expected by the financial adviser is also split in two:

- Generic administration – time spent on generic business activities such as accounting, FCA reporting, professional indemnity insurance applications, complaint handling, utility bills to pay, agency communications, fee collection and matching, ordering stationery, council tax bills, technology issues and training, etc.

- Client administration – time spent on client business activities that involve client-specific advice or ongoing support such as travelling to your client's meetings, time with your clients, research for clients, presentations to clients, implementation of client applications and client reports.

Client-specific support

When you advise a client for the first time, for example, to invest or save, this should be the start of a long-term relationship, but not the normal relationship you might expect of a client and their adviser. It should be a business relationship with a common objective, a partnership. The partnership should exist to ensure you work together to achieve an agreed goal. Each partner should have a role in the objective and be accountable to it.

In the last section, I wrote about the need to advise your clients about the importance of accumulating assets rather than spending. Spending disposable income on 'happy boost' products is always a short-term emotion – like drinking alcohol it provides a good feeling at the time, but a hangover afterwards. In contrast, saving will provide financial freedom to give happiness longer term. The secret is to achieve the short and long-term balance; enjoy life today but ensure you plan for the future too.

Your role as the adviser is to ensure your client, as the partner in the joint objective, is maintaining a balanced way of living so that they are both enjoying life and at the same time saving to accumulate assets. You may still be thinking, 'Ah, he means pension planning.' No, I mean accumulation of assets (not a product) that will produce an income today and not just in the future. Remember the wealthy, who only have assets with no need to work to generate income to live. It is their assets that produce the income with or without their input.

As partners in this venture, you have agreed a monetary asset accumulation target and identified their shortfall and objective. You each have a role in bridging this gap.

To help a client, and make a difference, is to ensure they understand that no amount of investment manipulation of their money, such as fund switching or taking more risk to obtain growth quicker, will make up the difference of their asset shortfall. They have to understand that the bulk of their shortfall will need to be met by their commitment to saving more and spend less. They need a goal to be happy.

> *"If you want to live a happy life, tie it to a goal. Not to people or things.'*
> **Albert Einstein**

Shortfalls to a target equate to many times a client's current savings. Supporting your client in reducing that deficit year on year is your role. There is no greater feeling of accomplishment than seeing a client's satisfaction when the savings gap is being bridged.

Take, for example, the effort athletes put in over a four-year period to not only compete at the Olympics but maybe to even win a medal, perhaps even Gold. All the effort and pain during training falls away from their memory when they achieve their goal. Equally, when your client achieves their savings target, with your help, support and guidance, it is you they will thank. They would not be happy if you failed to point out their shortfall in the first place.

While no one wants to hear they have a savings shortfall, by not highlighting the issue to your client you would be failing in your duty.

Paradoxically, your client may have excess over the target. Indeed, you could describe them as wealthy. They have no need for increased growth (unless they want their lifestyle to involve even more spending than they can currently afford on current asset income, in which case they are technically in shortfall). Wealthy clients have another issue; their estate is subject to taxation on death, so called inheritance tax.

Keeping inheritance tax issues simple, is achieved by gifting the excess over needs. This, like the savings gap above, requires a partnership between the adviser and the client. Rather than your client's commitment to saving and invest their money in bridging the savings gap, they instead work with you in reverse and gift their assets to their beneficiaries. The how, is about the product for the purpose but it is the commitment to act that you need to manage, monitor and support.

Non-client-specific generic business administration

This activity is not to be confused with client-specific administration and is typical of any business, not just financial services. All companies need accounts, stationery, IT hardware, internet connectivity, printers and replacement ink, vehicles, desk and office space. These are the core of any business and all are legitimate business expenses.

What is also in this category is the time and cost of self-development. Training needs or further qualifications are all part of the non-client generic business activity and administration. Some, such as continual professional development (CPD), are an industry demand.

These activities need to be time-managed and clearly set aside from your client-specific activity. The best way to ensure they remain separate is to set aside appropriate periods of the week for each activity and avoid crossover.

The simple way to identify one from the other is to ask yourself, 'Is this activity making me money or is it spending money?'

If you are making money, then it is through client-specific activity and related administration. If there is no money generated by the activity it's usually non-client-specific activity. Therefore, ensure you spend the minimal amount of time on non-client generic business administration and activity, or better still, outsource it.

Advisers need support

Even though times have changed with the welcome introduction of financial regulation to the advice industry, which set the industry in the right professional direction, many advisers simply don't do enough.

With good practice comes great rewards but with poor practice comes misery. Misery leads to blame and so the first thing for financial advisers to realise is that it is their own fault and no one else's.

Blaming the industry, the regulation or policy changes is all very well, but these changes happen to all financial advisers and many continue to thrive.

My aim is not to be merely critical, but in identifying your needless failings, I hope that financial advisers recognise their own failings and resolve to improve. Your happiness depends on improving standards by self-recognition and by your motivation to change and improve. However, I do recognise that adviser's today need support more than ever before, if they are to change and improve. My firm has that in place. If you are building a multi-adviser firm, you must ensure adviser support is a priority, or you will fail.

If you are willing to change, then the support is out there, but make sure it is in place for you before you embark on new ventures.

In the chapter on structure, the choice of developing your own multi-adviser firm or the more straightforward individual client-focused financial adviser (possibly within a multi-adviser firm) was offered. It is worth a note that multi-adviser or adviser-centred models fail because the principle founder of the firms cannot let go of their own clients. They hang on to their advice authorisation at all cost. Even a small selection of clients is too many. One is too many.

Apart from being paid, it is the support that self-employed advisers require more than anything else. Lack of support is a single enough reason for them to consider moving elsewhere. We recognise the importance of adviser support over and above that of system supply. They want to be able to pick up the phone and ask for support. That is why we have developed the Action Team Helpdesk. Advisers want answers quickly and efficiently. Our current group of advisers call us, on average, ten times each day with queries such as, system use, advice help, fee/commission payment and case checking, to name just a few. We support them, as they support their clients.

Developing a robust business plan takes an enormous amount of consideration, imagination, and diligence. Every moment should be focused on development and immediate constraints and let the advisers focus on their clients.

Training and competence

I recently attended a product development event in London, and it was suggested that I write down 100 silly mistakes my clients make. At the event, I could only come up with a few. On the three-hour train journey back to Carlisle, I astonished myself by identifying 104 mistakes or failings of a typical financial adviser. It was a great exercise in unlocking the grey matter and one I would recommend. It takes time to get a few but then it flows and I probably could have found a few more.

It is important that this list of 104 mistakes is not seen as being critical. In fact that list is not in this book, but in doing the task I have realised what is needed to eradicate such mistakes. Indeed, the opposite is needed. I have now compiled this list and reversed it and changed it into a strategy for good practice of a highly respected financial adviser – a purveyor of excellence in their field.

I have identified four key areas of support importance;

1   Client relationship support
2   Adviser Self-development support

3 Business efficiency support
4 Marketing effectiveness support

These support areas could be applied to any professional practice but is quite often missed by many in the financial advice world.

My aim is to educate financial advisers out there in good practice. To make the right progress, to plan before they promote and to ensure each decision has purpose. I have already spoken about client support, the importance of business efficiency and how time saved will impact on your new client marketing. But none of these factors will exist without high-quality adviser-specific support.

Adviser-specific support

Unlike other non-regulated businesses, financial advisers have a third administrative function governed by the authorities; on compliance, regulation and generic industry administration. Directly authorised firms tend to have their own staff for this activity or they outsource to other compliance firms, however the best system is to align with a company specifically set up to provide these services and support functions for you.

These companies deal with the regulatory burdens and agency relationships on your behalf. It is not easy to maintain over 180 agencies while trying to advise and support your clients, so joining a firm specifically so that it does that for you will allow you to focus on your clients.

Payment for support varies depending upon the level of support you require, so make sure you shop around, but the best firms are those who reconcile your fees for you and make regular payments into your account. Full records of these payments and reconciliations will also help you to prepare your annual accounts.

Adviser centered business models such as ours have no growth restrictions. The recruitment of an adviser anywhere in the UK is possible because of our technology; everything in the cloud. Our advisers come with their own clients in their own location, and we provide the brand, function, and support they need.

As we grow, we need to increase the support we offer to advisers. However, with any growth, we must ensure we don't deviate too far from our efficiency ratio.

Our business model is designed to expand efficiently (and significantly) at a ratio of ten advisers to one member of staff and that is the only constant to maintain. The only limit we have is our own ambition.

This ratio allows us to provide advisers with the support they need, yet maximise the returns on their fees. It's about creating the right balance.

For you to support your clients in achieving their targets you need to know there is a support function for you – a place with like-minded advisers who understand the industry and what you are trying to achieve. You will need an environment that takes away your business time so you can focus on helping your existing and new clients. You need someone or something to support you while you support your clients.

Happy Financial Advisers recognise the importance of compliance and active support as a protection facility, so they can focus on developing new business connections.

Directly authorised firms feel they have more control. However they are swamped with regulation so much that their time is absorbed with administration not linked to client advice or client support. In essence, the combination of running a small firm and advising clients are two roles that can be separated. While you advise your clients, let others deal with your agencies.

The support of your clients and the recording of that support (as required in today's post-RDR regulation) is all time-consuming. However, if you off-load the regulation element to a firm dedicated to the task, you will have the freedom to support your clients in achieving their goals. Further, coupled with the right use of technology in monitoring your clients progress, you will make more time to advise new clients.

Self-development skills

Happy Financial Advisers are never complacent and thrive on self-development and discovery. Like them, you should invest in yourself and work hard on improving ways to support your clients, efficiently of course. They recognise their need for support in all aspects of their improvement, especially embracing new ideas to help balance work and home lifestyle.

They are accountable for their own actions and doing nothing is never an option!

Happy Financial Advisers are hungry for knowledge and will set aside time to read articles or self- help books to increase their support and communication skills.

Ongoing training and mentoring

Happy Financial Advisers welcome a structure of ongoing training and support.

It is a common error in many business leaders, sole traders and entrepreneurs not to have a mentor. Can you imagine an Olympic athlete without a coach or mentor? The best sports people have coaches and mentors yet in business there tends to be few. Trust me, you don't know better and will always benefit from having a mentor!

If you have to pay for it, it's worth it.

It is important not to confuse a company support function that takes care of your regulatory or compliance concerns or maybe manages your agencies and pay reconciliation for you, with that of the mentor or coach who is there to support your own self-development. A mentor is usually an expert in a particular field, works impartially to your needs. A mentor is not a company.

For example, I have a business to run and that business supports financial advisers in such a way to ensure they and their clients are happy. But I also have a mentor of my own. Daniel Priestly is co-founder of Dent Global who supports entrepreneurs while they grow their business. He and his team have provided me with training on the right way to build my business that, I believe, provides me with an advantage over many competitors. Having a mentor is a business accelerator, and you too should have one.

The Dent Global website states,

> "We see a world where entrepreneurial teams are solving more meaningful problems. We believe that many businesses are standing on a mountain of untapped value and they have lost perspective on how to make the biggest dent in the universe. We know that less time struggling creates the capacity for people to deliver more value to the world. In addition to accelerating business success, we aim to inspire more companies to support the UN Global Goals through giving and innovation. Our vision is that business leaders

and entrepreneurs also measure success based on their ability to positively impact the world."

If you ignore this mentor idea then you will miss out on these seven benefits:

1 Mentoring generates improvements in your individual performance to achieve your personal goals by correcting poor behaviour and bad habits, removing performance difficulties
2 Mentoring increases your openness to pursuing personal learning and development
3 Mentoring will help you to identify solutions quickly to specific work-related issues
4 Mentoring provides greater ownership and confident responsibility
5 Mentoring develops self-esteem and self-awareness
6 Mentoring will improve a specific skill or behaviour
7 Mentoring provides greater clarity in your role and your life's objectives

Our approach to support

We provide new advisers with local mentoring support. From our vast experience, we know that in-the-field support is crucial to the long-term success of any financial adviser. Our mentoring approach is unique and allows an adviser's induction needs to be tailored specifically to them.

The training and mentoring are carried out by existing financial advisers in the firm which means there is always a high adviser-to-staff ratio, the benefit of which is an impressive cost saving. We distribute that saving to increase adviser pay, added value development and profit, all of which contributes to providing a happy environment. We are an off-the-shelf business that individual advisers can adopt quickly without fuss, yet with endless support.

What do mentors do?

They provide in-the-field support to the newly appointed adviser. Following the new adviser's initial induction course, the mentor will follow up soon after and ensure the adviser is settled back into their home workstation or local office and will offer advice and training. The mentor will be the first port of call for any new adviser who needs support while in transition.

Who are the mentors?

Our mentors are all existing IFAs within the firm, who have already achieved the company's minimum standards of advice, competence, and training. They will also be self-employed IFAs and have undergone additional training specifically focused to mentor new IFAs in or near their local area. They are not supervisors or managers but they are paid for their mentoring support.

What is the Action Team?

This is a team specifically set up to take new advisers from their induction course straight through to being signed off as a Truly Competent Adviser (TCAS). The team heads up company functions such as training, case checking, pre-approvals, mentoring, supervision and IFA support.

Can anyone become a mentor?

In short, yes. A mentor needs to satisfy minimum standards in all areas, be fully competent on IT systems and demonstrate loyalty to the firm. However, they also need to be living in or near an area of support. There are hence vacancies UK-wide to support our growth.

What other skills or standards does a mentor require?

To be a mentor, you need to:

- be a self-employed Truly Independent IFA
- hold the Truly Competent Adviser Status (TCAS) certificate
- be able to demonstrate our IT systems and hold a thorough knowledge of generic software such as email, Excel, Word, Yammer, product research, etc.
- be personable and patient

- be willing to respond quickly to requests for support
- be willing to travel and provide time to others
- be part of a team

Our business development mentors (consultants) will help you plan your transition and support you in the early months. They will help you to focus your time on the important business factors and ensure you consciously understand your transitional goals and how we can help you effectively achieve them.

Step 6. Succession
Prepare For Your Retirement

> '*One of the things we often miss in succession planning is that it should be gradual and thoughtful, with lots of sharing of information and knowledge and perspective, so that it's almost a non-event when it happens.*'
> **Anne M. Mulcahy**
> Former Chairman, and CEO, Xerox Corporation

Identify your buyer well in advance and don't rely on others to sell your business for you.

Succession planning is not just for the seller, but more importantly, is vital to the success of the buyer's business. Your business model must match that of the purchaser's, to fill their gap. With this in mind, it is wise for all sellers to communicate and connect with younger advisers and to keep up with new thinking, new ways, and new strategies. After all, your successor will most likely be someone you already know. Failing to identify a suitable buyer early, is failing to plan for both you and your buyer and could slow down your retirement plans.

The best business transfers are arranged in private. Any business transfer between two parties requires an equal understanding of what is being sold and what is being bought. Due diligence is essential but just as important is the integrity and preparation being exercised. With that in mind, I have created the acronym PREPARE to help you with your retirement and succession planning.

P – PLAN your retirement

Planning your retirement starts at the very beginning of your business, from day one. It should be in your business strategy to start with the end in mind. Your business plan is not just a plan for the coming year, it is also the plan that will eventually include the year you plan to retire, so ensure it is considered every day and year you are in business.

By now, you should have built a business that is both efficient and effective. Not having a business plan is not preparing to retire. A business that is very attractive to potential buyers which will command the best price. You have your business plan written and forever updated to be current. However, you are now in the retirement consideration mode, maybe with just a few years to plan your exit.

To plan well, you need to establish a target date to exit the industry fully. This should be at least three to five years ahead. If you wish to exit the industry at 65, then increase your preparation at age 60 and start planning; you have a lot to do, and remember, do not rely on others.

Here are six things to consider in your planning:

1 You need to be sure you are a ready to retire, as trial efforts simply waste time
2 You need to establish a list of potential buyers to target. Who and where are they?
3 You need to have a proposal or prospectus that outlines exactly what is on offer for sale.
4 You need to think about payment options for the buyer and have an agreement document template to sign.
5 You need to consider your exit strategy, either immediate or steady. How will you retreat?
6 You need to establish an absolute exit point to aim for.

R – RECKON your business

You have built your business and enjoyed the income it has generated over many years. You have planned and reviewed your business regularly and now have an extremely efficient and effective business to sell, allowing you to retire. The question is, are you ready to retire?

Reckon means you have reached the point that you are ready to evaluate and sell. You now want to exit absolutely. There is no longer a trial sale or consideration. From here on in, you are committed to sell and you are ready for the next stage of your preparation to exit from the industry, but what value do you place on your business?

Value

The idea of valuing your business purely as a multiple of recurring income is no longer a suitable or reliable method and is merely a 'hangover' from the days of commission. There is more to the value of your business than just the recurring figure. When arriving at a value, credence should be given for the following for each product area:

- Gross New Sales from existing clients
- Gross Sales from new clients, with a breakdown of the source:
  - Internet

- Website
- Unbiased.co.uk
- Find an Advisers searches
- Professional Introducers
  - Accountants
  - Solicitors
  - Business Network
- Direct marketing and adverts
- Referrals
  - From clients
  - From other Advisers
  - From Family or Friends

Your software should be able to provide this sort of data which can be used to enhance your proposition. Your ability to demonstrate a fuller understanding of your business to a potential buyer will increase the value.

Over the last five or ten years, far too much credibility has been placed on the present value of recurring income to value an IFA business. This may be fine if the buyer is paying a single lump sum payment with you taking immediate exit, after all, you would have no claim on the future business by taking a 100% buyout.

I predict that in the future, there will be more emphasis given towards new business opportunity and in particular, the source of that new business. It takes time to build a strong business with a focus on regular introductions and referrals from new clients. It is new clients the buyer is interested in, since they are looking to increase their opportunity and will place a greater value on established introducers and referrers than just existing renewal. The present value of your business is the future value of your business today and without the right data, you will be unable to predict that future value; so make sure you have the right systems and able to record the right data.

By definition, 'Future value is the value of an asset at a specific future date.' This means that you can measure the future value of your business, it's worth, at a specified time in the future, say three years ahead, assuming certain introductions of new business continues. More generally, if you can project a vision of your business with the use of graphs in a more formal prospectus, you will be able to use the anticipated future annual growth to achieve a better value today.

EXAMPLE

An adviser has a small business with £40,000 of recurring income plus new business from two accountancy introductions of £20,000 and existing client introductions of £10,000. Total turnover for the present year is therefore £70,000. He is willing to sell the business to a younger adviser over a 3 year payment period.

Using the traditional method, you may achieve 1.5 x recurring = £60,000. This may be acceptable for sale by lump sum purchase, but not suitable for 36 monthly installments; you may agree to receive £1,667 per month over 36 months to sell the business. However, this ignores the future value that future accountancy introductions will yield.

Using an alternative (future) method, you would include the worth of introductions to establish a future value. Hence after 3 years, the income would be £40,000 of original recurring income plus an estimated extra £18,000 of recurring income generated from the future introductions = £58,000.

That is 45% growth on recurring you would have lost. When this (future) figure of £58,000 is applied to the present 1.5 multiplier, the 36 monthly installments jump to £2,417per month.

How did we arrive at £18,000 extra?

- £30,000 of new income came from 2.5% initial charge of £1.2m of client investment
- This investment will increase recurring income at 0.5% by £6,000 per annum
- Purchase is over 3 years, so 3 x £6,000 = £18,000

Of course, your own charging structure may differ and you will need to take account of that in your own future value formula. The point is, you will be able to sell your business over a three year period, which will favour more buyers and provide you with more sale opportunities.

It's all in the presentation. When someone says, "I sold my business for £150,000", they don't mean someone rang them out of the blue and offered them some money. They mean they *sold* their business. You need to get your business in order ready for sale, then produce an enticing document to demonstrate its future value to your buyer.

You then need to identify your buyer and sell your business to them.

E – ESTABLISH potential buyers

Retiring from the financial advice business may at first appear to be a frightening consideration. This (in part) is due to the perceived loss of regular income that advisers are used to. When asking advisers for their main concern it is typically the affordability question. Equally, clients will also need to know what happens to them when their adviser retires, which is a consideration of longevity missed by many advisers.

So, how best does an adviser identify a buyer for their business?

Agencies

It is possible to find an agency to sell your business for you but that will come at a price. Here are five reasons not to rely on their marketing or expertise:

1 They are not interested in achieving the best price for you, since quite often they will be acting initially for both parties by bringing them together.

2 They will charge both parties a completion fee which has known to be as high as 6% on both sides.

3 They are not interested in regular monthly instalments, since they will want their fee on completion only.

4 As the one-off seller, you will not bring repeat business for them so they don't have your interest at heart.

5 They will not spend any time with you to establish a process or methodology for sale.

If you have to rely on an agency to sell your business then you have failed to plan, to prospect and promote your business.

Until 31st December 2012, the retirement option was exactly that, an option, however, the retail distribution review (RDR) revised qualification rules resulted in the forced deauthorisation of experienced advisers. For many (up to 20% of advisers) the retirement option was removed and retirement became compulsory when new qualification levels were not achieved. Equally, under new fee contracts it is not easy to sell your business *en bloc* as it once was. Hence an alternative to sale at retirement is needed that we have cultivated as a realistic and proven alternative.

P – PRESENT your prospectus to your potential buyers

Having established potential buyers, you should present your business to them for their interest and invite offers. Contact with prospects should be a verbal presentation supported with your written proposal, especially aimed at your buyer to read and appraise. Your proposal should include:

- A brief biography of yourself
- Information about your clients and their locations or areas of distribution
- The breakdown of business type of pension, investment, protection and mortgage
- Your last twelve months business figures with breakdown details of sources – existing, new or introduced.
- Your last three years accounts in table form
- Your projections of the business three to five years ahead, using past variables.
- Timetable to retirement and proposed purchase agreement
- Contact details.

A – AGREE terms with your buyer

Review your business proposal with your intended buyer. This should be a joint exercise to help build the relationship. It could take over two years to complete the purchase, less or more, depending upon your planned time to retire fully.

The agreement is verbal initially and then written to be agreed, signed and witnessed by a third party. The agreement should include:

- What is being sold and what is being purchased
- The purchase price
- The purchase period
- Any guarantees

R – RETREAT from your business

Having agreed on terms and signed the necessary agreements, it is time to transfer your business, clients and other assets to your buyer.

To ensure a smooth transition, you need to ensure your clients understand the succession process and so ensuring your buyer is able to take over where you left off without a break in activity, smooth enough that clients cannot see the seam.

Following the signing of your agreement, your retreat covers both the time you take to exit and your activity in that withdrawal of services. Your retreat period should not be too long or too short. Retreating should involve the handover of your business to your buyer for the benefit:

1 Of your clients to smooth and alleviate any concerns
2 Of your buyer:
   a To help cement client relationships and
   b To aid any financial constraints via an affordable purchase plan
3 Of your own retirement realisation

E – EXIT the industry

Take the time you need to retire, but when you do, make sure you exit fully. Plan a long overdue round the world trip – you deserve it!

Exit is not just about closing the door behind you. You need to make sure:

- you have been fully paid for the business
- you have no outstanding issues that need your attention
- you have no overhanging future complaints or surprises
- you inform your regulator of your exit
- you inform your clients of your final exit day and their future contact

Our approach to succession

There is an alternative. One option that we have developed is to match a retiring adviser (retiree) with a level 4 qualified truly independent adviser (successor) in a two-stage acquisition process. Working together, there is a natural blend of experience and qualifications where all parties can benefit, even the client.

Your successor will support you in your retirement and we can even provide a local mentor for you to work with. Our contracts and successor agreements ensure smooth and uncontested relationships. Of course, you may already have a successor in mind.

Working together, as the retiree, generating such income in retirement does not just happen without input. It is about ensuring both parties (the retiree and the successor) work together in harmony and a pre-agreed transition period:

- communicate regularly with each other (and clients)
- be fair to each other, as business partners
- set targets and make them joint ventures
- identify and agree a marketing strategy
- ensure the activities agreed are reviewed and improved
- identify and agree each other's role or roles
- enjoy the change and enjoy the challenge

This type of succession strategy ensures your clients receive continuity of available advice and ongoing support without any disruptive transitions typical of a business sale. Equally, you can maintain the opportunity to receive income in your retirement at a level equivalent to your net recurring income for up to four years (or other agreed time period).

At the end of your agreed period, you can happily exit the industry... maybe with a pina colada on the beach!

Final Thoughts
And Making It Happen

Like the Happy Financial Adviser, you should choose to be happy and not rely on others to make it so. You should recognise that happiness should not be treated as some future emotion as a result of a successful purchase, a car, a house or a holiday, and that happiness can be achieved today with a little change of attitude, direction and determination.

You should appreciate that in order to be happy, you must embrace technology and social media to connect with more people. Actively taking part in local associations, groups and charities will enhance your life and create opportunities to meet new clients.

You must engineer your freedom from restricted business models, and take the truly independent route. Seek help and support to maximise your time and minimise constraints to within touching distance of the boundary that is regulation. You should efficiently, as the industry can allow, ensure you remain effective in business.

You must make sure you are making a positive difference in the lives of your clients by encouraging a focus on the achievement of financial goals through a client/adviser joint venture to accumulation assets and not to dwell on product or policy discussions. Make sure your client commits to the challenge of saving while you monitor their progress to bridge the savings gap, or to minimise inheritance tax through lifetime gifting.

Like the Happy Financial Adviser, you should now understand the difference between three core barriers to your happiness. The historical timeline that has determined todays regulation and resulting PII interference along with current and future policy changes are here to stay. They are barriers to speed and demand great patience. They are the barriers you must tolerate. Accept compliance as an essential part of a robust client proposition in a complex business.

Like the Happy Financial Adviser, you should realise that regulation and RDR has reduced financial adviser numbers, leaving a huge opportunity for those accepting of change. There is huge opportunity to fill the advice gap and this is best done as an independent financial adviser with the backing of advanced technology to compete against the future that is Robo-advice.

Like the Happy Financial Adviser, you should take responsibility for your own actions and outcomes, blaming no others. In ensuring this, you should aim to develop skills beyond those already achieved.

You should welcome new beginnings and build on the right structures and strategy that will progress you into a new financial advice world that builds confidence and credibility.

Like the Happy Financial Adviser, you need to embrace a better way of living on a daily basis. Instead of being stressful, work more efficiently to make more time for you to be healthier. Find time to connect with your family, community and new clients.

Your Call To Action

When you have decided that you want a lifestyle adviser business and wish to avoid the often long, difficult process of the start-up pitfalls of disappointment and sacrifice, then consider running your lifestyle adviser business through the umbrella company Truly Independent Ltd.

We offer our advisers a truly independent lifestyle adviser business model that allows you to take control of your own time without the worry of premises, staff, managers or the administrative burden of regulatory relationships.

For more information go to
www.happyfinancialadvisers.co.uk
and request a no obligation discovery session with one of
our existing IFA and Business Development Mentors.

About Truly Independent Ltd

Truly Independent Ltd® is a national firm of experienced independent financial advisers who provide a traditional method of face-to-face independent financial planning advice.

Launched in 2010, their aim is to distance themselves from other traditional financial adviser firms by fully embracing and promoting the magic of advanced modern technology and to redefine 'independence'.

For more information go to www.trulyonline.co.uk

Acknowledgements

In an Edinburgh bar, a friend of mine said to my son, 'The one thing about your dad is, he is always happy.' I am a happy man – I have a wonderful wife and amazing son and together we share good times and create great memories. To Catherine and Thomas, I love you both very much.

I have great friends too from school days, university days and from my time at General Accident, Positive Solutions; all hilarious friends I have had the good fortune to meet and have supported and encouraged me to write and shares good times.

I would especially like to thank my business partner, friend and co-founder of Truly Independent Ltd, Cath Bowden who has kept the engine running, allowing me to focus on business development. Thank you to Neil Jeffrey who has shown faith in us both. Thanks go to all at Truly, our IFAs and staff for their contributions in a great firm. Equally to the handful of early investors, clients and friends who saw the vision.

Special acknowledgements go to two brilliant mentors and business confidants without whom my business ideas and this book would not exist – David Harrison and Daniel Priestley: you are inspirational. Thanks for the support we have had from all at True Potential and Dent

Global. Equally, thank you to Lucy McCarraher and Joe Gregory at Rethink press.

A special thank you to my dad Raymond Goodwin for offering your own determination to succeed which I have inherited, for your ear and your encouragement to be both happy and brave; we've had fun times.

Last, and by no means least, a heartfelt thank you to Sylvia Henry for your support when we needed it most.

You all deserve to be happy.

The Author

Andrew Goodwin is the Managing Director and Co-founder of national IFA, Truly Independent Ltd.

His twenty-year career in financial services started when he graduated from Heriot-Watt University in Edinburgh with an honours degree in actuarial mathematics and statistics.

Between 1995 and 2003 he worked for General Accident (now Aviva) as a Senior Financial Consultant before moving into their corporate division where he achieved advanced qualifications in Taxation & Trusts, Supervision & Sales Management and Pensions.

In 2004 he joined national IFA, Positive Solutions, on a self-employed contract and during this period he recruited and mentored others into a similar role. By 2008 he was head of the north division in charge of his own recruitment team of business consultants.

In 2009, he recognised that the industry was changing and left Positive Solutions to set up his own multi-adviser firm, with co-founder Cath Bowden, called Truly Independent Ltd. With an initial investment of just £10,000 Truly Independent Ltd today is one of the largest IFA firms in the country.To learn more about Andrew, go to:

www.happyfinancialadvisers.co.uk/blog
www.linkedin.com/in/andrew-goodwin-3466a062/
www.twitter.com/trulyifa

Lightning Source UK Ltd.
Milton Keynes UK
UKOW05f0742070517

300633UK00009B/104/P